SENSUAL ALIEN ENCOUNTERS

Ken Hudnall
Omega Press
El Paso, TX

SENSUAL ALIEN ENCOUNTERS
COPYRIGHT © 2015 KEN HUDNALL

All rights reserved. No part of this book may be reproduced or transmitted in any form or by any means, graphic, electronic, or mechanical, including photocopying, recording, taping or by any information storage or retrieval system, without the permission in writing from the publisher.

OMEGA PRESS

An imprint of Omega Communications Group, Inc.

For information contact:

Omega Press

5823 N. Mesa, #839

El Paso, Texas 79912

Or http://www.kenhudnall.com

FIRST EDITION

Printed in the United States of America

OTHER WORKS BY THE SAME AUTHOR UNDER THE NAME KEN HUDNALL FROM OMEGA PRESS

MANHATTAN CONSPIRACY SERIES
Blood on the Apple
Capitol Crimes
Angel of Death

THE OCCULT CONNECTION
UFOs, Secret Societies and Ancient Gods
The Hidden Race
Flying Saucers
UFOs and the Supernatural
UFOs and Secret Societies
Evidence of Alien Contact
UFOs and Ancient Gods

DARKNESS
When Darkness Falls
Fear The Darkness

SPIRITS OF THE BORDER
(with Connie Wang)
The History and Mystery of El Paso Del Norte
The History and Mystery of Fort Bliss, Texas

(with Sharon Hudnall)
The History and Mystery of the Rio Grande
The history and Mystery of New Mexico
The History and Mystery of the Lone Star State
The History and Mystery of Arizona
The History and Mystery of Tombstone, AZ
The History and Mystery of Colorado
Echoes of the Past
El Paso: A City of Secrets
Tales From The Nightshift

The History and Mystery of Sin City
The History and Mystery of Concordia

THE ESTATE SALE MURDERS
Dead Man's Diary

Northwood Conspiracy

No Safe Haven; Homeland Insecurity

Where No Car Has Gone Before

Seventy Years and No Losses: The History of the Sun Bowl

How Not To Get Published

Vampires, Werewolves and Things that Go Bump in the Night

PUBLISHED BY PAJA BOOKS
The Occult Connection: Unidentified Flying Objects

DEDICATION

As with all of my books, I could not have completed this book if not for my lovely wife, Sharon.

TABLE OF CONTENTS

BIBLICAL CLUES TO RACE MANIPULATION
                                         9

HUMAN ORIGINS   19

THE NEANDERTHAL MYSTERY   25

THE ANNUNAKI, THE WATCHERS AND THE IGIGI   31

WE LEARNED FROM THE GODS   47

THE FALL OF SUMERIA AND THE RISE OF AKKADIA   67

BABYLONIA/EGYPT/INDIA   75

ENCOUNTERS BETWEEN GODS AND HUMANS   89

BIBLICAL ENCOUNTERS   109

MORE EVIDENCE OF INTERACTION   125

ALIEN DESCRIPTIONS   135

A BREEDING PROGRAM	153
A BLOODY FASCINATION	167
BILL ENGLISH AND GRUDGE 13	185
FINAL ANALYSIS	211
INDEX	215

CHAPTER ONE

BIBLICAL CLUES TO RACE MANIPULATION

There have been many questions about whether or not the human race has had contact with alien races. In the Bible there is discussion about the sons of God having sexual intercourse with the daughters of man. The results of these interactions between races were called the Nephilim.

The Nephilim were offspring of the "sons of God" and the "daughters of men" before the Deluge according to Genesis 6:4; the name is also used in reference to giants who inhabited Canaan at the time of the Israelite conquest of Canaan according to Numbers 13:33. A similar biblical

Hebrew word with different vowel-sounds is used in Ezekiel 32:27 to refer to dead Philistine warriors[1].

The Brown-Driver-Briggs Lexicon gives the meaning of Nephilim as "giants"[2]. Many suggested interpretations are based on the assumption that the word is a derivative of Hebrew verbal root n-ph-l "fall". Robert Baker Girdlestone[3] argued the word comes from the Hiphil causative stem, implying that the Nephilim are to be perceived as "those that cause others to fall down". Adam Clarke took it as a perfect participle, "fallen", "apostates". Ronald Hendel states that it is a passive form "ones who have fallen", equivalent grammatically to paqid "one who is appointed" (i.e., overseer), asir, "one who is bound", (i.e., prisoner) etc[4]. According to the Brown-Driver-Briggs Lexicon, the basic etymology of the word Nephilim is "dub[ious]", and various suggested interpretations are "all very precarious"[5].

The majority of ancient biblical versions, including the Septuagint, Theodotion, Latin Vulgate, Samaritan Targum, Targum Onkelos and Targum Neofiti, interpret the

---

[1] Wikipedia
[2] Brown Driver Briggs Hebrew Lexicon p. 658; Strongs H5307
[3] Girdlestone R. Old Testament Synonyms p. 54
[4] Hendel R. ed. Auffarth Christoph; Loren T. Stuckenbruck The Fall of the Angels Brill (22 Feb 2004)
[5] Brown Driver Briggs Hebrew Lexicon p. 658

word to mean "giants"[6]. Symmachus translates it as "the violent ones[7]" and Aquila's translation has been interpreted to mean either "the fallen ones" or "the ones falling [upon their enemies]". The nature of the Nephilim is complicated by the ambiguity of Genesis 6:4, which leaves it unclear whether they are the "sons of God" or their offspring who are the "mighty men of old, men of renown". Richard Hess in The Anchor Bible Dictionary takes it to mean that the Nephilim are the offspring, as does P. W. Coxon in Dictionary of Deities and Demons in the Bible[8].

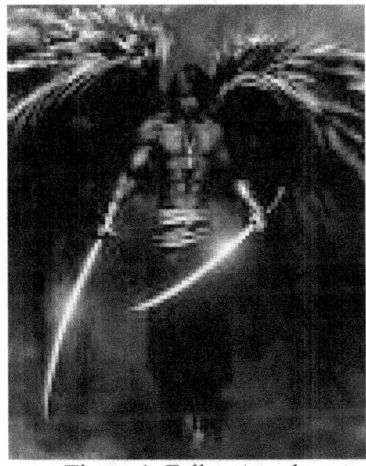

Figure 1: Fallen Angels

As we wrote in UFOs and Ancient Gods[9], there are numerous legends of ancient gods interacting with early man to create civilization and all of its wonders. Of course, there are as many who believe that the ancient

---

[6] Van Ruiten, Jacques (2000). Primaeval History Interpreted: The Rewriting of Genesis I-II in the Book of Jubilees
[7] Wright, Archie T. (2005). The Origin of Evil Spirits: The Reception of Genesis 6.1-4 in Early Jewish Literature
[8] P. W. Coxon, article "Nephilim" in K. van der Toorn, Bob Becking, Pieter Willem van der Horst, "Dictionary of deities and demons in the Bible
[9] Hudnall, Ken, UFOs and Ancient Gods, Omega Press, El Paso, Texas 79912 (2014)

gods were just myths and make believe. Others believe that these ancient gods were actually aliens who came to this planet to exploit it for its natural resources. The question is did the gods create mankind or did the gods come to exploit a pre-existing mankind?

FALLEN ANGELS

We all know the story in the Christian Bible of when God cast out 1/3 of his angels from heaven to earth because they had joined Lucifer in a rebellion against God. These fallen angels were called the Nephilim in the Bible and interbred with human females, which shows that the "gods" and humans were related.

If Zacharia Sitchin was correct and the Annunaki were space travelers who came to earth to exploit it for its riches, the so called fallen angels were rebellious space men who decided to take advantage of the locals. This would not be the first time that primitives mistook advanced beings and technology as something coming from the gods. Prime examples of this concept were the Cargo Cults found in the Pacific during and after World War II. The primitive tribesmen of the area found crashed cargo planes and viewed what was on them as riches sent by the gods. A religion grew up around the idea that such riches came from the gods and praying to them would keep the flow of goods coming.

Figure 2: St. Michael leading the hosts of Heaven

In their rights, the Sumerians claimed that gods came from the heavens above and taught them many works and wonders of life. The chief teacher for the Sumerians was called Oannes and was said to be half fish and half man. The Sumerians accurately recorded and described our galaxy and every planet within it down to the colors, textures, rotations, and locations of them. How would they know all of this information about other planets?

The Sumerians claim that Gods from above, "the enlightened ones," came down from the "heavens" and taught them many arts. This sounds very much like God's fallen angels may have come to earth and taught many secrets to mankind and portrayed themselves as Gods in their own right. These Gods would come and go as they please into and out of our planet. Or perhaps, these superior beings were space travelers? Actually, these being have many things in common with our modern day aliens. Think about all the ancient Gods recorded through-out our history. Could all those civilizations who claimed to know and walk with these Gods just be plain crazy or perhaps there is truth in what they said?

Another theory, which has a lot to be said for it is that current civilization was based on a much older advanced civilization that was destroyed by some cataclysm. The "gods" who roamed the planet and taught early man may well have been survivors of this early civilization and imparted their secrets to early man. This would account for the stories of early man walking and talking with the "gods".

Of course there are also stories that the gods of earth were survivors of a war in the heavens. But not all are familiar with the war that broke out in heaven, when it was said that Jesus cleansed the heavens of Satan and his demons and casted them down to the earth. The Christian Bible's Book of Revelation describes a "war in heaven" between angels led by the Archangel Michael versus those led by "the dragon", identified with "the devil and Satan", which were defeated and thrown down to the earth. Could this planet have been used as a prison for these defeated warriors?

Revelation's "war in heaven" has been compared to the idea of fallen angels and possible parallels have been proposed in the Hebrew Bible and Dead Sea Scrolls. The Bible says that Satan keeps transforming himself into an angel of light and many people claim to have seen angels of light today as well. Those who favor this theory believe that the idea of Aliens actually comes from Satan. These same fanatics say that anything that is not found in Almighty God's word comes from Satan, as a result of this narrow minded attitude the truth is hidden from sight.

Under this theory, every time someone was "supposedly" being abducted by aliens, and they prayed to the Lord to protect them, it was said that the aliens would disappear. If you ever watch these "alien abductions" shows, you'll see the same thing. The few people who cried out to the Lord are said to have found that the abduction stopped. How much of this was real and how much was an attempt on the part of the entities to support the idea of religious intervention? From a practical standpoint, religion is a fantastic control mechanism as anything taboo as contrary to the religion of the time is safe from discovery by the vast majority of the population.

Scientists who do their research from their own private ivory towers believe that abductees suffer from sleep paralysis and they are imagining that they are being attacked at night. These victims of so called alien abduction see all kinds of things from aliens to old hags, a mysterious dark man and others of the same ilk. Some of those who believe that they are actually abducted report being held down not being able to speak.

The origin of demons is not commonly known in our time. However, in ancient times it was well understood that demons are the disembodied spirits of the Nephilim. The reader will recall that the Nephilim (the earth-born giants of the days of Noah) were the offspring of what were described as fallen angels and the 'daughters of men.'

Figure 3: There are many stories about UFOs in ancient Egypt.

According to numerous ancient

rabbinic and Early Church texts, when the Nephilim died their spirits became disembodied and roamed the earth, harassing mankind.

Mysterious teachers, strange aerial craft and other things we would call UFO events have been with us for thousands of years, however, there are many who choose to place the beginning of the modern UFO phenomenon at the point of pilot Kenneth Arnold's sighting in 1947 (which many prefer to do), there is nevertheless a direct relationship between UFOs and the fallen angels, and stories of encounters with angels handed down through the scriptures of many religions, and some of the arguments in favor of the angelic interpretation of ancient and modern UFO accounts. It interesting to note that most people regard angels as existing in a spiritual plane only, however, Angels (fallen or not) exist in both the physical and spiritual planes.

According to the Bible, so rife were the Nephilim and their own offspring, along with Satan's offspring which had polluted the gene pool of man eons earlier, that only Noah was pure in his ancestry and so God sent the flood. Now, the fallen angels are once again loose on the Earth, and once again mixing their DNA with ours.

CHAPTER TWO

HUMAN ORIGINS

There has been much talk and research conducted by archaeologists, anthropologists and others who seek to determine where man may have originated. Whatever their field of study, there is no question that mainstream scientists all profess to believe that man was created (or developed) and progressed along a steady timeline where each change or improvement to the species happened over millennia. However, what if this is not true? What if the human race has been selectively modified and guided over millions of years? As we progress through this work, you will see that there is a large body of evidence which supports this premise.

There is even some belief that early man may well have been decidedly different from modern man. One example is the belief that primitive humans are thought to have b4een more telepathic before the development of language by prehistoric tribes. This would explain much in the development of those we refer to as psychics. They merely retain more of their ancestor's abilities than the norm. This is certainly possible. I trying to determine how the human race developed, William H. McNeil made the observation in his book *The Rise of the West: A History of Human Community*[10] that *"how modern types of men originated is one of the unsolved puzzles of archaeology and psychical anthropology. Cultural evolution must have begun among the pre-human ancestors of modern man."*

For those who choose to throw dogma out the window (there are certain avenues within these fields of study that are considered forbidden as they do not follow the orthodox premises laid down within each scientific field) serious research will also reveal that there have been many instances of what can only be viewed as paranormal events that have had a decided impact on the human race.

---

[10] McNeil, William H., *The Rise of the West: A History of Human Community,* (New York: Mentor, 1963)

Accepted Theory

Figure 4: Homo Habilis

According to accepted theory, mankind's "ancestor apes" were probably present on Earth as long as twenty-five million years ago. The evolution to hominids or manlike apes occurred perhaps fourteen million years ago.

Approximately two million years ago the first beings that could be described as homo or manlike appeared in Africa. These very early manlike creatures were called Homo Habilis.

Figure 5: Homo Erectus

A million years ago we see the appearance of *Homo Erectus.* About 900,000 years later we see the appearance of the first being that has been classified as "primitive man." This primitive man we call Neanderthal Man.

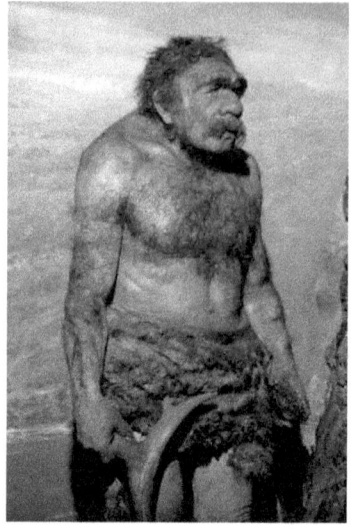

Figure 6: Neanderthal Man

Mainstream science posits that between the appearance of the first manlike creature and *Neanderthal man* was some two million years. However, in spite of this time span, both the "manlike creature" and Neanderthal man looked alike and used similar stone tools. Why the long time span you may ask? Well, logically changes that eventually appeared in modern man could not have happened over night; therefore, a couple of million years was needed. However, what if this is not true?

Figure 7: Cro-Magnon Man

But to continue discussing accepted theory, we next see Homo sapiens appearing about 35,000 years ago. What distinguished Homo sapiens from Neanderthal man you may ask? Well, it was the ability to think. These thinking Homo sapiens were called *Cro-Magnons* and looked very much like modern man physically. This timeline is well and good, but it does raise some interesting questions. For example what happened to Neanderthal man once the Cro-Magnon Man appeared? Once one looks behind the curtain, so to speak, it is clear that there are a number of mysteries involving the development of the human race. From the evidence it seems relatively clear that the development of early man and the move toward organized civilization was influenced, if not guided, by outside forces. Let's look more deeply into that question.

CHAPTER THREE

THE NEANDERTHAL MYSTERY

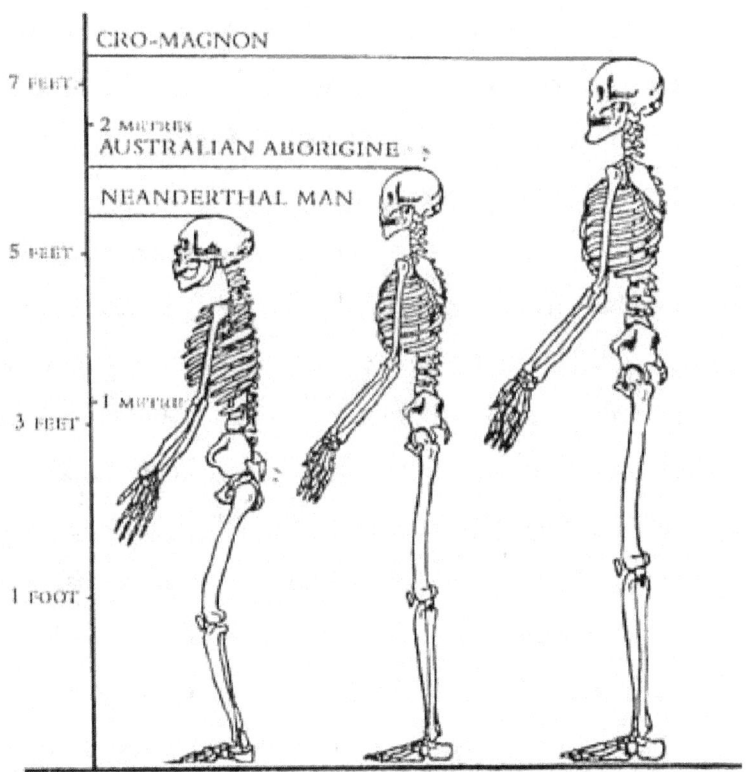

Figure 8: Differences between Neanderthal and Cro-Magnon

According to accepted scientific theory, Neanderthal man had dominated the planet for a couple of million years. If that was the case, why did they disappear, so to speak, after the arrival of Cro-Magnon Man? It makes no logical sense. If Neanderthal man was older, bigger, stronger and better adapted to the environment as evidence indicates, why did it simply fade away after the appearance of Home Sapiens?

In fact, it makes about as much sense as stating that man descended from apes. If this was the case, then why are there not new specifies of human being created all of the time, since Apes still exist today? There is certainly a missing element to the theorizing.

One theory to explain the disappearance of the Neanderthal man is that they "somehow" vanished as a species and Homo sapiens replaced Neanderthal until the older species was extinct. Certainly, there is no archaeological evidence that the two species interbred, which is a major puzzle in itself. Why did they not interbreed? The only answer would be if Neanderthal as a species was sterile. We know that Homo sapiens "went forth and multiplied" so there was no sterility there. But this theory is impossible as Neanderthal existed for a couple of million years and unless they were immortal had to be mating among themselves. If the two species were related, as science has said for eons, then interbreeding between the two species would be possible and, knowing the propensity of modern man to "wander", mating was very likely if not certain to occur. So what could explain the disappearance of Neanderthal man as a species?

Actually, more recent archaeological evidence suggests that Neanderthals and Cro-Magnons cohabited the planet for some time, during which time the two species may well have mated. Certainly, in North America, archaeological evidence shows that Homo sapiens first surfaced in the New World around 10,000 B.C. However, McNeil[11] noted in his book that even the skeletal characteristics of the first inhabitants of America were unusual, or unclear, as he stated. So it would appear that there was some, perhaps, limited mating between the two species which would explain unusual, or unclear, skeletal characteristics.

More Mysteries

Author Zacharia Sitchin[12] discussed the evolution of man in his series of books that he called the Earth

---

[11] Ibid
[12] Sitchin, Zacharia, *The 12th Planet* (Rochester, Vermont: Bear & Company, 1976)

Chronicles. As he observed, *"It is clear that Homo sapiens represent such an extreme departure from the slow evolutionary process that many of our features, such as the ability to speak, are totally unrelated to the earlier primates."* So it is clear to those not steeped in classical archaeological and anthropological thinking that our ancestors appeared long before they should have on the evolutionary scale. This insightful observation supported Sitchin's own theory that life as we know was imported from elsewhere.

Another mystery relates to how Homo sapiens became the most adaptable of all species. Though smaller and less robust than Neanderthal man, Homo sapiens were, by far, the more long lasting species which actually makes no sense. However, as McNeil[13] noted, *"all details of human evolution are uncertain."* This statement alone is mind blowing. If the Darwin's Theory is correct, why would details of evolution be uncertain? Another mystery.

---

[13] McNeil, William H., *The Rise of the West: A History of Human Community*, (New York: Mentor, 1963)

Figure 9: Accepted Human Evolution

A study of genetics makes it clear that the offspring has characteristics of both of the parents. Thus, it becomes a mystery as to how Homo Erectus became Neanderthal and how Neanderthal became Cro-Magnon. Each species has some characteristics not found in the parents. For this reason many researchers believe that there was some outside intervention in the development of the human race as we know it.

I have heard discussions of recessive traits, junk DNA and almost every other possible idea to explain how a species can mutate. However, the bottom line is that before a change can take place in the makeup of a species there must first be some outside intervention. This idea brings us to the ancient astronaut theory, or some variation thereof.

Even the early Sumerians talked extensively about being taught by a creature that came from the sea called Oannes. Oannes was said to have taught them the rudiments of civilization, interacting with the people on a daily basis.

This brings to mind Sitchin's discussion of the fact that there were more male Annunaki than there were female. Taking into consideration the Biblical notation that the Nephilim took the daughters of m an as their mates and produced offspring, it is clear that there was some sexual advantage taken by these visitors. The question becomes how extensive was this exploitation and frankly, is it still going on today.

CHAPTER FOUR
THE ANNUNAKI, THE WATCHERS AND THE IGIGI

Figure 10: An Annunaki as describ3ed by ancient records

This was discussed in Evidence of Alien Contact[14] in much more detail. The Anunnaki[15] (also transcribed as: Annunaki, Anunna, Anunnaku, Ananaki and other variations) are a group of deities in ancient Mesopotamian cultures (i.e. Sumerian, Akkadian, Assyrian, and Babylonian). The name is variously written "da-nuna", "da-nuna-ke4-ne", or "da-nun-na",

---

[14] Hudnall, Ken, Evidence of Alien Contact, Omega press, El Paso, TX 79912 (2014)
[15] See the work of Zacharia Sitchin entitled "The Earth Chronicles".

meaning something to the effect of "those of royal blood" or "princely offspring". According to The Oxford Companion to World Mythology, the Anunnaki "are the Sumerian deities of the old primordial line; they are chthonic deities of fertility, associated eventually with the underworld, where they became judges. They take their name from the old sky god An[16] (Anu).

Their relation to the group of gods known as the Igigi[17] is unclear – at times the names are used synonymously but in the Atra-Hasis flood myth the Igigi are the sixth generation of the Gods who have to work for the Anunnaki, rebelling after 40 days and replaced by the creation of humans.

Jeremy Black and Anthony Green[18] offer a slightly different perspective on the Igigi and the Anunnaki, writing that "Igigu or Igigi is a term introduced in the Old Babylonian Period as a name for the (ten) "great gods". While it sometimes kept that sense in later periods, from Middle Assyrian and Babylonian times on it is generally used to refer to the gods of heaven collectively, just as the term Anunnakku (Anuna) was later used to refer to the

---

[16] The original King of the Gods
[17] According to Sitchin, the Igigi are those referred to as the Watchers.
[18] Black, Jeremy and Green, Anthony: Gods, Demons and Symbols of Ancient Mesopotamia: An Illustrated Dictionary University of Texas Press (Aug 1992)

gods of the underworld. In the Epic of Creation it is said that there are 300 lgigu in heaven."

The Anunnaki appear in the Babylonian creation myth, Enuma Elish. In the late version magnifying Marduk, after the creation of mankind, Marduk divides the Anunnaki and assigns them to their proper stations, three hundred in heaven, three hundred on the earth. In gratitude, the Anunnaki, the "Great Gods", built Esagila, the splendid: "They raised high the head of Esagila equaling Apsu. Having built a stage-tower as high as Apsu, they set up in it an abode for Marduk, Enlil, and Ea." Then they built their own shrines.

The Annunaki are mentioned in The Epic of Gilgamesh when Utnapishtim tells the story of the flood. The seven judges of hell are called the Annunaki, and they set the land aflame as the storm is approaching. Clearly the Annunaki were looked at as extremely powerful.

According to later Assyrian and Babylonian myth, the Anunnaki were the children of Anu and Ki, brother and sister gods, themselves the children of Anshar and Kishar (Skypivot and Earthpivot, the Celestial poles), who in turn were the children of Lahamu and Lahmu ("the muddy ones"), names given to the gatekeepers of the Abzu (House of Far Waters) temple at Eridu, the site at which the creation was thought to have occurred. Finally, Lahamu and Lahmu were the children of Tiamat (Goddess of the Ocean) and Abzu (God of Fresh Water).

There are also stories in the various religious works about the watchers. Watcher is a term used in connection with biblical angels. Watcher occurs in both plural and singular forms in the Book of Daniel (2nd century BC), where reference is made to their holiness. The apocryphal Books of Enoch (1st and 2nd centuries BC) refer to both good and bad Watchers, with a primary focus on the rebellious ones. These watchers were said to be assigned to watch the earth and keep track of what the humans were up to. Others say that the Watchers may well be the Igigi, assigned to stay on board the base craft of the Annunaki expedition. Interestingly enough when man first went into space an unknown orbiting craft was found in a polar orbit. It was named the Black Knight and is rarely spoken of by those in authority.

There is a great deal of information to be found about the Watchers in the Book of Enoch, an early religious tract about a man named Enoch and his travels and travails. There were actually two books called the Book of Enoch[19].

---

[19] The Book of Enoch, Oxford: Clarendon, 1893, reprinted in 1895. Republished by Boston, MA: Samuel Weiser; 2003. ISBN 1-57863-259-5

In the Book of Enoch[20], the Watchers are referred to as angels dispatched to Earth to watch over the humans. They soon begin to lust for human women and, at the prodding of their leader Samyaza, defect enmasse to illicitly instruct humanity and procreate among them. The offspring of these unions are the Nephilim, savage giants who pillage the earth and endanger humanity. Samyaza and his associates further taught their human charges arts and technologies such as weaponry, cosmetics, mirrors, sorcery, and other techniques that would otherwise be discovered gradually over time by humans, not foisted upon them all at once. Eventually God allows a Great Flood to rid the earth of the Nephilim, but first sends Uriel to warn Noah so as not to eradicate the human race. The Watchers are bound "in the valleys of the Earth" until Judgment Day. (Jude verse 6 says that these fallen angels are kept "in everlasting chains under darkness" until Judgment Day.)

The chiefs of tens of these fallen angels also listed in the Book of Enoch are as follows:

And these are the names of their leaders: Sêmîazâz, their leader, Arâkîba, Râmêêl, Kôkabîêl, Tâmîêl, Râmîêl, Dânêl, Êzêqêêl, Barâqîjâl, Asâêl, Armârôs, Batârêl,

---

[20] The Book of Enoch or 1 Enoch: Translated from the Editor's Ethiopic Text, Oxford: Clarendon, 1912.

Anânêl, Zaqîêl, Samsâpêêl, Satarêl, Tûrêl, Jômjâêl, and Sariêl[21].

The book of Enoch also lists leaders of the 200 fallen angels who married and commenced in unnatural union with human women, and who taught forbidden knowledge. Some are also listed in Book of Raziel (Sefer Raziel HaMalakh), the Zohar and Jubilees.

- Araqiel (also Arakiel, Araqael, Araciel, Arqael, Sarquael, Arkiel, and Arkas) taught humans the signs of the earth. However, in the Sibylline Oracles, Araqiel is referred to not as a fallen angel, or Watcher, but as one of the 5 angels who lead the souls of men to judgment, the other 4 being Ramiel, Uriel, Samiel, and Azazel.
- Armaros (also Amaros) in Enoch I taught men the resolving of enchantments.
- Azazel taught men to make knives, swords, shields, and how to devise ornaments and cosmetics.
- Gadreel taught the art of cosmetics, the use of weapons and killing blows. It was he who led Eve astray in the Garden of Eden.
- Baraqel (Baraqiel) taught men astrology
- Bezaliel mentioned in Enoch I, left out of most translations because of damaged manuscripts and problematic transmission of the text.
- Chazaqiel (sometimes Ezeqeel or Cambriel) taught men the signs of the clouds (meteorology).

---

[21] R. H. Charles translation, The Book of the Watchers, Chapter VI.

- Kokabiel (also Kakabel, Kochbiel, Kokbiel, Kabaiel, and Kochab), In the Book of Raziel he is a high-ranking, holy angel. In Enoch I, he is a fallen Watcher, resident of the nether realms, and commands 365,000 surrogate spirits to do his bidding. Among other duties, he instructs his fellows in astrology.
- Penemue "taught mankind the art of writing with ink and paper," and taught "the children of men the bitter and the sweet and the secrets of wisdom." (I Enoch 69.8)
- Sariel (also Suriel) taught mankind about the courses of the moon (at one time regarded as forbidden knowledge).
- Samyaza (also Shemyazaz, Shamazya, Semiaza, Shemhazi, Semyaza and Amezyarak) is one of the leaders of the fall from heaven in Vocabulaire de l' Angelologie.
- Shamsiel, once a guardian of Eden as stated in the Zohar, served as one of the two chief aides to the archangel Uriel (the other aide being Hasdiel) when Uriel bore his standard into battle, and is the head of 365 legions of angels and also crowns prayers, accompanying them to the 5th heaven. In Jubilees, he is referred to as one of the Watchers. He is a fallen angel who teaches the signs of the sun.
- Yeqon (also Jeqon or Yaqum, "he shall rise") was the ringleader who first tempted the other Watchers into having sexual relations with humans. His accomplices were Asbeel, Gadreel, Penemue, and

Kasdaye (or Kasadya). Together, they were known as the Five Satans.

The account of the Book of Enoch has been associated with the passage in Genesis 6:1-4, which speaks of Sons of God instead of Watchers:

> *When men began to multiply on earth and daughters were born to them, the sons of God saw how beautiful the daughters of man were, and so they took for their wives as many of them as they chose. Then the Lord said: "My spirit shall not remain in man forever, since he is but flesh. His days shall comprise one hundred and twenty years." At that time the Nephilim appeared on earth (as well as later), after the sons of God had intercourse with the daughters of man, who bore them sons. They were the heroes of old, the men of renown.*
> —Genesis 6:1-4

Second Book of Enoch
For the masculine given name, see Grigori (given name) and Grigory

The Jewish pseudepigraphon Second Book of Enoch (Slavonic Enoch) refers to the Grigori, who are the same as the Watchers of 1 Enoch. The Slavic word Grigori used in the book is a transcription of a Greek word in post-classical times, meaning "wakeful".

Chapter 18 presents the Grigori as countless soldiers of human appearance, "their size being greater than that of great giants[22]". They are located in the fifth heaven and identified as "the Grigori, who with their prince Satanail rejected the Lord of light". One version of 2 Enoch adds that their number was 200 myriads. Furthermore, some "went down on to earth from the Lord's throne" and there married women and "befouled the earth with their deeds", resulting in confinement under earth. The number of those who descended to earth is generally put at three, but Andrei A. Orlov, while quoting the text as saying three, remarks in a footnote that some manuscripts put them at 200 or even 200 myriads.

Chapter 29, referring to the second day of creation, before the creation of human beings, says that "one from out the order of angels" or, according to other versions of 2 Enoch, "one of the order of archangels" or "one of the ranks of the archangels conceived an impossible thought, to place his throne higher than the clouds above the earth, that he might become equal in rank to [the Lord's] power. And [the Lord] threw him out from the height with his angels, and he was flying in the air continuously above the bottomless."

---

[22] This could be the basis for the race of giants discovered in North America – See U.F.O.s and Ancient Gods, by Ken Hudnall.

Although in this chapter the name "Satanail" is mentioned only in a heading added in one manuscript, this chapter is often understood to refer to Satanail and his angels, the Grigori.

The Mercer Dictionary of the Bible makes a distinction between the Grigori and the fallen angels by stating that in fifth heaven, Enoch sees "the giants whose brothers were the fallen angels." The longer recension of 2 Enoch 18:3 identifies the prisoners of second heaven as the angels of Satanail.

Much of what we known about the Annunaki came from the research of Zacharia Sitchin. He has long been the major investigator of the Sumerian records dating from the earliest days of Sumerian civilization. Zechariah Sitchin[23] believes that his work shows that many of the Biblical Stories of gods and angels originated from Sumeria and the activities of the Annunaki.

---

[23] Zecharia Sitchin (July 11, 1920 – October 9, 2010) was an Azerbaijani-born American author of books proposing an explanation for human origins involving ancient astronauts. Sitchin attributes the creation of the ancient Sumerian culture to the Anunnaki, which he states was a race of extraterrestrials from a planet beyond Neptune called Nibiru. He believed this hypothetical planet of Nibiru to be in an elongated, elliptical orbit in the Earth's own Solar System, asserting that Sumerian mythology reflects this view. Sitchin's books have sold millions of copies worldwide and have been translated into more than 25 languages.

Further, he claims that the Annunaki were on Earth about 450,000 years ago, primarily looking for gold which was very important in their culture, and perhaps for their longevity. This gold prospecting was said to have originally taken place in Africa and as we shall see there is much evidence to support this premise.

Not surprisingly, such advanced beings in ships and with 'magical' technology were viewed as gods by the primitive humans. The main person was Anu who was in charge overall and probably remained in his ship in orbit around Earth.

Beneath him were Ninhursag, Enlil (brother and sister) and Enki, as well as Marduk, Inanna and a variety of minor deities each with their own areas of responsibility.

From careful reading of the clay tablets and interpretation of the carvings on the cylinder seals found in ancient Sumer, Sitchin has pieced together a detailed history of the Annunaki which he believed showed that our history was not the true history of this planet.

The full story is very long and worth reading if you

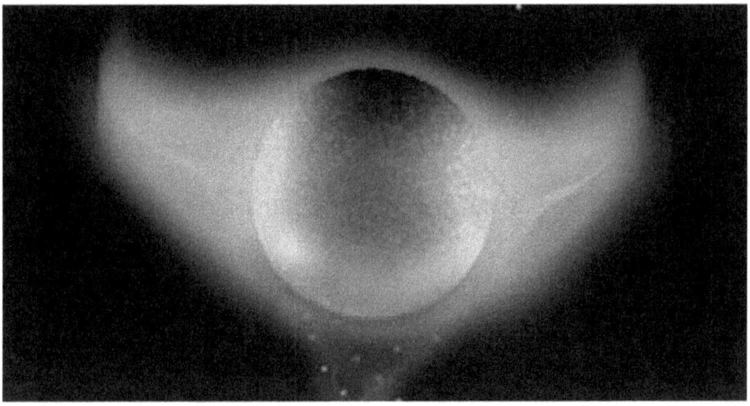

Figure 11: Planet X or Nibiru

are at all interested in this aspect of alien intervention in human affairs. There are six books in his series titled 'The Earth Chronicles'. In them, he takes the story of the Annunaki from their origin on another planet (which has since been known as Nibiru, Planet X, Marduk and The Twelfth Planet), and tells of how they mined gold, manipulated the genes of humanity and generally altered the normal run of affairs on Earth.

For example, there is a puzzling passage in Genesis chapter 6 verse 4 which reads; "*There were giants in the earth in those days; and also after that, when the sons of God came in unto the daughters of men, and they; bare children unto them, the same became mighty men which were of old, men of renown.*"

A different version has that same passage as, "*The Nephilim were upon the Earth in those days and thereafter too. Those sons of the gods who cohabited with the daughters of the Adam, and they bore children into them. They were the Mighty Ones of Eternity, the People of the Shem.*"

This could be explained as the Annunaki coming down from above and co-habiting with human women. Instead of giants, the term 'Fallen Ones' is better explained by their descent from the heavens in their ships. The Nephilim were, according to Sitchin, the Annunaki.

All this is, of course, interesting. But the main interest to me is the influence these aliens have had upon us.

Look at the civilization of Sumer as a start. This advanced culture seemingly sprang up overnight from a gaggle of simple primitives. This new civilization bore the hallmarks of an aware and technologically capable society at a time when no-one can point to any possible precursor. Taxes, irrigation,

Figure 12: Sumerian Frieze

public buildings, a powerful priesthood, a civil code, factories, all of these trapping of a complex society just appeared pretty much out of nowhere. If that isn't having an influence on us, I'd like to know what is!

For example, if we were bred to be slaves of a kind, isn't it interesting that we have the same attitude to our animals? We breed them with little thought to their emotions, feelings, desires or anything else. We impose our desires on them, much as the Annunaki imposed theirs on us.

And what of the strange fixation we have with adornments, precious metals and sex? If the records are exact, then these same traits were those of the aliens. They enjoyed gold jewelry. They altered us to be able to have sex and produce all the time (not the norm!), and they generally showed us the way to behave...belligerently, with little regard to others and to concentrate on outward show rather than inward meaning.

Now, I know these are huge generalizations, but the traits we exhibit as humans must have come from somewhere. I do not subscribe to the theory that these are natural developments of evolution. They are, in many ways, unnatural. Additionally, there is the question of giants, the wee people and the monsters of legend. Could the aliens who created mankind have created the other races of myth and legend? I think it is the case. And we have the Annunaki to thank for them...for us!!

CHAPTER FIVE

WE LEARNED FROM THE GODS

Figure 13: Ancient Egyptian God Sobek

So what is the evidence that ancient aliens interfered in human development? Well frankly, nothing physical that can be pointed to as made on Mars or some other place in outer space. However, we do have many stories told by our ancestors that directly state that the gods taught man the rudiments of civilization. This should be enough to prove the case, correct. Unfortunately this is not true.

Each of the three early civilizations in the Middle East talked of mysterious teachers and in South Ame4rica there was the mysterious Quetzalcoatl who walked the continent teaching the arts of civilization. Unless we presuppose an initial, as yet unknown advanced civilization on earth, we must therefore look to the stars for these teachers.

Figure 14: The Serpent people

Historians, archaeologists and anthropologists all consider such stories as superstitious nonsense. However, let us explore the evidence and see if we get a different conclusion. One thing that most of these scientists (there is nothing that "all" scientists agree with) agree with is that over 6,000 years ago the world's first great civilization was Sumer located in Mesopotamia. For those not familiar with Sumer, it was called Chaldea in the Bible. Mesopotamia, which was located between the Tigris and the Euphrates rivers, is known today as Iraq.

The Sumerian civilization existed for over 2,000 years and had a huge impact on the world. Unfortunately, it disappeared as inexplicably as it appeared. So who were the Sumerians and where did they come from?

Sumer

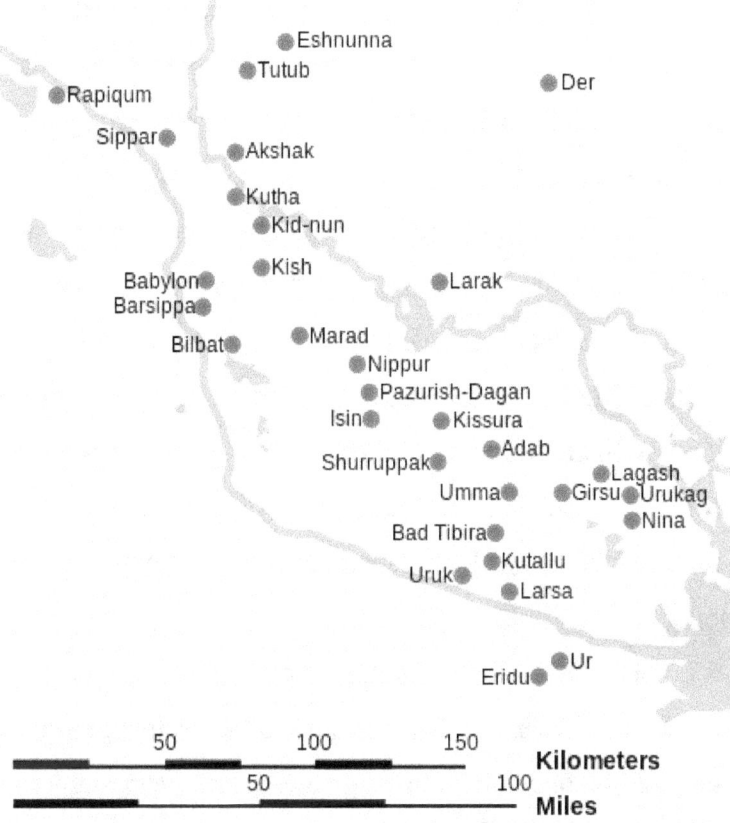

Figure 15: Cities of ancient Sumer

There is not a tremendous amount of information known about this early civilization. Sumeria was one of the ancient civilizations and historical regions in southern Mesopotamia, modern-day southern Iraq, during the

Chalcolithic and Early Bronze Age[24]. Although it was previously thought that the earliest forms of writing in the region do not go back much further than c. 3500 BC, modern historians have suggested that Sumer was first permanently settled between c. 5500 and 4000 BC by a non-Semitic people who spoke the Sumerian language (pointing to the names of cities, rivers, basic occupations, etc. as evidence)[25].

These conjectured, prehistoric people are now called "proto-Euphrateans" or "Ubaidians"[26], and are theorized to have evolved from the Samarra culture of northern Mesopotamia (Assyria)[27]. The Ubaidians were the first civilizing force in Sumer, draining the marshes for agriculture, developing trade, and establishing industries, including weaving, leatherwork, metalwork, masonry, and pottery.

However, some scholars such as Piotr Michalowski and Gerd Steiner, contest the idea of a Proto-Euphratean language or one substrate language. It has been suggested

---

[24] http://en.wikipedia.org/wiki/Sumer
[25] "Ancient Mesopotamia. Teaching materials". Oriental Institute in collaboration with Chicago Web Docent and eCUIP, The Digital Library.
[26] "Sumer (ancient region, Iraq)". Britannica Online Encyclopedia. Britannica.com
[27] Kleniewski, Nancy; Thomas, Alexander R (2010-03-26). "Cities, Change, and Conflict: A Political Economy of Urban Life". ISBN 978-0-495-81222-7.

by them and others, that the Sumerian language was originally that of the hunter and fisher peoples, who lived in the marshland and the Eastern Arabia littoral region, and were part of the Arabian bifacial culture. Reliable historical records begin much later; there are none in Sumer of any kind that have been dated before Enmebaragesi (c. 26th century BC).

Professor Juris Zarins believes the Sumerians were settled along the coast of Eastern Arabia, today's Persian Gulf region, before it flooded at the end of the Ice Age[28]. Sumerian literature speaks of their homeland being Dilmun.

Sumerian civilization took form in the Uruk period (4th millennium BC), continuing into the Jemdat Nasr and Early Dynastic periods. During the 3rd millennium BC, a close cultural symbiosis developed between the Sumerians (who spoke a language isolate) and the Semitic Akkadian speakers, which included widespread bilingualism.

The influence of Sumerian on Akkadian (and vice versa) is evident in all areas, from lexical borrowing on a massive scale, to syntactic, morphological, and phonological convergence. This has prompted scholars to refer to Sumerian and Akkadian in the 3rd millennium BC

---

[28] Hamblin, Dora Jane (May 1987). "Has the Garden of Eden been located at last?" (PDF). Smithsonian Magazine

as a Sprachbund[29]. Sumer was conquered by the Semitic-speaking kings of the Akkadian Empire around 2270 BC (short chronology), but Sumerian continued as a sacred language. Native Sumerian rule re-emerged for about a century in the Third Dynasty of Ur (Sumerian Renaissance) of the 21st to 20th centuries BC, but the Akkadian language also remained in use.

Figure 16 Sumerian City of Eridu as it was believed to have appeared

The Sumerian city of Eridu, on the coast of the Persian Gulf, was the world's first city, where three separate cultures fused — that of peasant Ubaidian farmers, living in mud-brick huts and practicing irrigation; that of mobile nomadic Semitic pastoralists living in black tents

---

[29] Deutscher, Guy (2007). Syntactic Change in Akkadian: The Evolution of Sentential Complementation. Oxford University Press US

and following herds of sheep and goats; and that of fisher folk, living in reed huts in the marshlands, who may have been the ancestors of the Sumerians.

The irrigated farming together with annual replenishment of soil fertility and the surplus of storable food in temple granaries created by this economy allowed the population of this region to rise to levels never before seen, unlike those found in earlier cultures of shifting cultivators. This much greater population density in turn created and required an extensive labor force and division of labor with many specialized arts and crafts. At the same time, historic overuse of the irrigated soils led to progressive salinization, and a Malthusian crisis which led to depopulation of the Sumerian region over time, leading to its progressive eclipse by the Akkadians of middle Mesopotamia.

Sumer was also the site of early development of writing, progressing from a stage of proto-writing in the mid-4th millennium BC to writing proper in the 3rd millennium BC.

Evidence of wheeled vehicles appeared in the mid-4th millennium BC, near-simultaneously in Mesopotamia, the Northern Caucasus (Maykop culture) and Central Europe. The wheel initially took the form of the potter's wheel. The new concept quickly led to wheeled vehicles and mill wheels. The Sumerians' cuneiform writing system is the oldest (or second oldest after the Egyptian hieroglyphs) which has been deciphered (the status of even older inscriptions such as the Jiahu symbols and Tartaria tablets is controversial). The Sumerians were among the first astronomers, mapping the stars into sets of constellations, many of which survived in the zodiac and were also recognized by the ancient Greeks. They were also aware of the five planets that are easily visible to the naked eye.

They invented and developed arithmetic by using several different number systems including a mixed radix system with an alternating base 10 and base 6. This sexagesimal system became the standard number system in Sumer and Babylonia. They may have invented military formations and introduced the basic divisions between infantry, cavalry, and archers. They developed the first known codified legal and administrative systems, complete with courts, jails, and government records.

The first true city-states arose in Sumer, roughly contemporaneously with similar entities in what are now Syria and Lebanon. Several centuries after the invention of cuneiform, the use of writing expanded beyond debt/payment certificates and inventory lists to be applied for the first time, about 2600 BC, to messages and mail delivery, history, legend, mathematics, astronomical records, and other pursuits. Conjointly with the spread of writing, the first formal schools were established, usually under the auspices of a city-state's primary temple.

Finally, the Sumerians ushered in domestication with intensive agriculture and irrigation. Emmer wheat, barley, sheep (starting as mouflon), and cattle (starting as aurochs) were foremost among the species cultivated and raised for the first time on a grand scale.

It was also discovered that the Sumerian civilization had remarkable celestial knowledge far beyond anything one would expect in an ancient culture. It is also said that the Sumerians inexplicable understood spherical astronomy including the 360 degree circle. This is simply unbelievable.

Based on the above it is clear that the Sumerians literally appeared from nowhere and proceeded to establish an advanced civilization. The question becomes where did they gain the knowledge? No one seems to know. However, the Sumerians made no secret about it; they were taught by the gods.

What Do We Know?

It was not until the 1840s that archaeologists discovered the buried remains of Sumerians cities as well as thousands of clay tablets written in the original Sumerian wedge-shaped cuneiform language. Until these discoveries, skeptics believed that Sumer had never existed. As research continued and graves were found, scientist was in for an even bigger shock. When skeletal remains were examined, the Sumerians bore no physical resemblance to other civilizations or tribes in that part of the world. No did their language resemble anything ever seen before. So who were the Sumerians?

There have been a number of theories offered to explain who the Sumerians were. Alan and Sally Landsburg, coauthors of *In Search of Ancient Mysteries*[30] wrote that the Sumerians "*pop up like some devilish jack-in-the-box around 3,000 B.C.*". They went on to suggest that the Sumerians were extraterrestrial colonists possessed of technology advanced well beyond our own today.

In 2000 Jim Marrs wrote *Rule by Secrecy*[31] in which he reasoned that an explanation for their advanced

---

[30] Landsburg, Alan and Sally, *In Search of Ancient Mysteries*, (New York: Bantam Books, 1974)
[31] Marrs, Jim, *Rule By Secrecy* (New York: Harper Collins, 2000)

knowledge might come from the Sumerians themselves. He suggested looking to see who they said taught them. The Sumerians themselves wrote that *"everything they achieved came from their gods."*

Figure 17: Zacharia Sitchin

Most scholars look at such statements as mythology, noting that all primitive societies had a belief system that included gods who come down to Earth from somewhere above. However, the real question becomes who were these gods and when and how did they arrive on this planet?

Zacharia Sitchin conducted much research regarding this belief of the Sumerian people. In his book *12th Planet,*[32] he wrote that *"Earth was indeed visited in the past by astronauts from another planet. Was life imported to Earth from elsewhere?"*

The Sumerians built massive cities, including substantial temples for devotion to the gods, known as

---

[32] Sitchin, Zacharia, *The 12th Planet* (Rochester, Vermont: Bear & Company, 1976)

"temple communities', but interestingly enough they never applied the term gods to whoever brought them their advanced knowledge[33]. Rather the Sumerians called their teachers the Annunaki[34]. <u>*By this distinction, the Sumerians were saying that their teachers came from the skies but they were not gods.*</u>

In his works, Zacharia Sitchin discussed his belief that these Annunaki came from another planet to Earth, mated with the local inhabitants and thus created a more advanced Human species that would otherwise have been possible. This theory actually has support from no less an authority than the Holy Bible. In Genesis, the text refers to the "Giants in the Earth" later referred to as the Nephilim, whose daughters married the children of Adam and Eve[35].

As Sitchin and others have pointed out in the Old Testament there are references to the Nephilim. This word has been traditionally translated as giant. In actuality in ancient Sumerians the word translates as *"those who were case down."*

---

[33] McNeil, William H., T*he Rise of the West: A History of Human Community*, (New York: Mentor, 1963)
[34] The term Annunaki was translated from the original Sumerian language as "those who came to Earth from Heaven."
[35] Notice from the comparison chart in Chapter Two that Cro-Magnon man could well be referred to as a giant being over 7 feet tall.

In the Old Testament Book of Genesis, it is written that *"the Nephilim were on earth in those days and also afterward when the sons of God went to the daughters of men and had children by them. They were the heroes of old, men of renown."*

The Holman Bible Dictionary defines the Nephilim as *"ancient heroes who according to most interpretations are the products of sexual union of heavenly beings and human women."* It would seem that the Sumerians were discussing this long before the Biblical texts.

Sitchin concluded that at several points during ancient times extraterrestrials brought both their seed as well as technology to Earth which would explain the mystery of ancient Sumerians civilizations beginnings and their tremendous accomplishments. It should also be remembered that the Sumerians said that the Annunaki came from the 12th planet in our solar system, called Nibiru[36].

According to Sitchin's research the Ancient Sumerians were able to correctly identify the planets Uranus, Neptune and even Pluto (only discovered by our scientists in 1930). It would seem that the Sumerians were very sophisticated in their astronomy which would tend to

---

[36] Nibiru has also been referred to as Marduk

support their belief that there was one more planet in our solar system[37].

It is interesting to note that the great Sumerian civilization lasted only about 2,000 years and then mysteriously vanished[38]. To date, there has been no answer to this question. It is as if the entire civilization just simply packed up and left, much as did the Maya in South America. Could there be a connection?

The Teachers

The knowledge that led to Sumer becoming a major power in a short period of time had to come from somewhere. According to the earliest legends of this planet, found in almost every early civilization on the planet that man was raised by a god, or gods, from his primitive state to become what he (or she) is today. Now comes the question, who were these gods? According to the Sumerians man was created in the laboratory by the Annunaki[39] to be a worker drone. Either an intention

---

[37] Sitchin, Zacharia, *The 12th Planet* (Rochester, Vermont: Bear & Company, 1976)

[38] Mellresh, M. L., The Sumerians (New York: Crowell, 1965)

[39] According to later Babylonian myth, the Annunaki were the children of Anu and Ki, brother and sister gods, themselves the children of Anshar and Kishar (Skypivot and Earthpivot, the Celestial poles), who in turn were the children of Lahamu and Lahmu ("the muddy ones"), names given to the gatekeepers of the Abzu temple at Eridu, the site at

modification or a lab accident gave man the ability to procreate.

Christianity talks about the Hebrew god who created the world in six days and rested on the seventh. Of course even the biblical books seem to have some confusion regarding this concept. God is said to be the one true god, but the word used to describe him in the original Hebrew works use the word Elohim. This word is used to refer to the one god and yet Elohim is a Hebrew word which expresses concepts of divinity or deity, notably used as a name of God in Judaism. It is apparently related to the Northwest Semitic word Ēl which means "god". Within the Hebrew language however, Elohim is morphologically a plural, in use both as a true plural with the meaning "angels, gods, rulers" and as a "plural intensive" with singular meaning, referring to a god or goddess, and especially to the single God of Israel[40].

But Christianity is not the only religion that uses language that refers to the concept of one God actually being "gods". The ancient Sumerians talk about the creature that came from the sea to teach their remote ancestors the arts of civilization. In the *Earth Chronicles*

---

which the creation was thought to have occurred. Finally, Lahamu and Lahmu were the children of Tiamat and Abzu.
[40]Wikipedia

series, author Zacharia Sitchin outlined the writings of the ancient Sumerians. According to his translations, the Sumerians believe that they were taught the rudiments of civilization by a being called Oannes.

Oannes was actually the name given by the

Figure 18: Oannes

Babylonian writer Berossus in the 3rd century BC to a supposedly mythical being who is said to have taught early mankind (Sumer) wisdom. Berossus describes Oannes as having the body of a fish but underneath it was said that he had the figure of a man. This being is described as dwelling beneath the waters of the Persian Gulf. According to the Sumerian writings Oannes rose out of the waters in the daytime and furnished mankind instruction on writing, the arts and the various sciences.

The name "Oannes" was once conjectured to be derived from that of the ancient Babylonian god Ea, but it is now known that the name is the Greek form of the Babylonian Uanna (or Uan) a name used for Adapa[41] in texts from the Library of Ashurbanipal[42]. The Assyrian texts attempt to connect the word to the Akkadian for a craftsman ummanu but this is a merely a pun. Scholars have long speculated that the name might ultimately be

---

[41] Adapa was a mortal from a godly lineage, a son of Ea (Enki in Sumerian, a name specifically applied to one of the leaders of the Annunaki), the god of wisdom and of the ancient city of Eridu, who brought the arts of civilization to that city (from Dilmun, according to some versions). He broke the wings of Ninlil the South Wind, who had overturned his fishing boat, and was called to account before Anu. Ea, his patron god, warned him to apologize humbly for his actions, but not to partake of food or drink while he was in heaven, as it would be the food of death. Anu, impressed by Adapa's sincerity, offered instead the food of immortality, but Adapa heeded Ea's advice, refused, and thus missed the chance for immortality that would have been his.
Adapa is often identified as advisor to the mythical first (antediluvian) king of Eridu, Alulim. In addition to his advisory duties, he served as a priest and exorcist, and upon his death took his place among the Seven Sages or Apkallū. (Apkal, "sage", comes from Sumerian Abgallu (Ab=water, Gal=Great, Lu=man) a reference to Adapa, the first sage's association with water.)

[42] Ashurbanipal (Akkadian: Aššur-bāni-apli, "Ashur is creator of an heir"; 685 B.C. – c. 627 B.C.), also spelled Assurbanipal or Ashshurbanipal, was the son of Esarhaddon and the last great king of the Neo-Assyrian Empire (668 B.C. – c. 627 B.C.). He established the first systematically organized library in the ancient Middle East, the Library of Ashurbanipal, which survives in part today at Nineveh. In the Bible he is called Asenappar (Ezra 4:10).[4] Roman historian Justinus identified him as Sardanapalus

derived from that of the 8th century figure of Jonah (Hebrew Yonah). Bible critics have made the reverse claim, although the Hebrew name has the known meaning of "dove". Oannes has historically been portrayed as a man wearing the skin of a fish. Or is it perhaps a man, or perhaps Alien, wearing a diving suit? It is a mystery, but some knew the truth.

In fact, each early civilization on this planet talked about a mysterious being that came from nowhere to teach the locals the rudiments of civilization. In each case, once the civilization began to grow in sophistication, the teacher mysteriously vanished into the mists, never to be seen again. Suffice it to say without these mysterious teachers civilization on this planet might be very different.

But now comes some big questions, who were these teachers, where did they come from and where did they go? Of course there is the biggest question of all, were these mysterious teachers who raised the human race from the primitive jungle runners to be civilized actually the gods of antiquity?

In earlier eons, depending on your belief, God, or the gods, dealt directly with man, or at least certain representatives of man. During this same era, God, or one or more of the gods, had relations with human females and gave birth to entities part god and part mortal. These were the famous demi-gods who became the rulers of lesser mortals. These were the sons of the gods. The gods themselves seem to have pulled away from man, to oversee things from afar. So what happened? Why did the gods leave?

CHAPTER SIX

THE FALL OF SUMERIA AND THE RISE OF AKKADIA

Nature a vacuum so as Sumeria faded in history, there arose a new power, Akkadia. The Akkadian Empire was an ancient Semitic empire centered in the city of Akkad and its surrounding region, also called Akkad in ancient Mesopotamia. The empire united all the indigenous Akkadian-speaking Semites and the Sumerian speakers under one rule. The Akkadian Empire grew to control Mesopotamia, the Levant, and parts of Iran.

During the 3rd millennium BC, there developed a very intimate cultural symbiosis between the Sumerians and the Semitic Akkadians, which included widespread bilingualism. Akkadian gradually replaced Sumerian as a spoken language somewhere around the turn of the 3rd and the 2nd millennia BC (the exact dating being a matter of debate).

The Akkadian Empire reached its political peak between the 24th and 22nd centuries BC, following the conquests by its founder Sargon of Akkad (2334–2279 BC). Under Sargon and his successors, Akkadian language was briefly imposed on neighboring conquered states such as Elam. Akkad is sometimes regarded as the first empire in history, though there are earlier Sumerian claimants.

After the fall of the Akkadian Empire, the Akkadian people of Mesopotamia eventually coalesced into two major Akkadian speaking nations: Assyria in the north, and, a few centuries later, Babylonia in the south. The Empire of Akkad collapsed in 2154 BCE, within 180 years of its founding, ushering in a Dark Age period of regional decline that lasted until the rise of the Third Dynasty of Ur in 2112 BC.

By the end of the reign of Naram-Sin's son, Shar-kali-sharri (2217–2193 BC), the empire had weakened. There was a period of anarchy between 2192 BC and 2168 BC. Shu-Durul (2168–2154 BC) appears to have restored some centralized authority, however he was unable to prevent the empire eventually collapsing outright from the invasion of barbarian peoples from the Zagros Mountains known as the Gutians.

Little is known about the Gutian period, or how long it endured. Cuneiform sources suggest that the Gutians' administration showed little concern for maintaining agriculture, written records, or public safety; they reputedly released all farm animals to roam about Mesopotamia freely, and soon brought about famine and rocketing grain prices. The decline coincided with severe drought, possibly connected with climatic changes reaching all across the area from Egypt to Greece. The Sumerian king Ur-Nammu (2112–2095 BC) cleared the Gutians from Mesopotamia during his reign.

It has recently been suggested that the regional decline at the end of the Akkadian period (and of the First Intermediary Period that followed the Ancient Egyptian Old Kingdom) was associated with rapidly increasing aridity, and failing rainfall in the region of the Ancient Near East, caused by a global centennial-scale drought. H. Weiss et al. have shown "Archaeological and soil-stratigraphic data define the origin, growth, and collapse of Subir, the third millennium rain-fed agriculture civilization of northern Mesopotamia on the Habur Plains of Syria. At

2200 B. C., a marked increase in aridity and wind circulation, subsequent to a volcanic eruption, induced a considerable degradation of land-use conditions. After four centuries of urban life, this abrupt climatic change evidently caused abandonment of Tell Leilan, regional desertion, and collapse of the Akkadian empire based in southern Mesopotamia. Synchronous collapse in adjacent regions suggests that the impact of the abrupt climatic change was extensive." Peter B. deMenocal, has shown "there was an influence of the North Atlantic Oscillation on the stream flow of the Tigris and Euphrates at this time, which led to the collapse of the Akkadian Empire".

The Sumerian King List, describing the Akkadian Empire after the death of Shar-kali-shari, states:

"Who was king? Who was not king? Irgigi the king; Nanum, the king; Imi the king; Ilulu, the king—the four of them were kings but reigned only three years. Dudu reigned 21 years; Shu-Turul, the son of Dudu, reigned 15 years. ... Agade was defeated and its kingship carried off to Uruk. In Uruk, Ur-ningin reigned 7 years, Ur-gigir, son of Ur-ningin, reigned 6 years; Kuda reigned 6 years; Puzur-ili reigned 5 years, Ur-Utu reigned 6 years. Uruk was smitten with weapons and its kingship carried off by the Gutian hordes.

However, there are no known year-names or other archaeological evidence verifying any of these later kings of Akkad or Uruk, apart from a single artifact referencing king Dudu of Akkad. The named kings of Uruk may have been contemporaries of the last kings of Akkad, but in any event could not have been very prominent.

The king list of the Gutian hordes is as follows:
- (first reigned) a nameless king; (then)
- Imta reigned 3 years as king;
- Shulme reigned 6 years;
- Elulumesh reigned 6 years;
- Inimbakesh reigned 5 years;
- Igeshuash reigned 6 years;
- Iarlagab reigned 15 years;
- Ibate reigned 3 years;
- (unknown) reigned 3 years;
- Kurum rained 1 year;
- (unknown) reigned 3 years;
- (unknown) reigned 2 years;
- Iararum reigned 2 years;
- Ibranum reigned 1 year;
- Hablum reigned 2 years;

- Puzur-Sin son of Hablum reigned 7 years;
- Iarlaganda reigned 7 years;
- (unknown) reigned 7 years;
- (unknown) reigned 40 days.

Total 21 kings reigned 91 years, 40 days.

Evidence from Tell Leilan in Northern Mesopotamia shows what may have happened. The site was abandoned soon after the city's massive walls were constructed, its temple rebuilt and its grain production reorganized. The debris, dust and sand that followed show no trace of human activity. Soil samples show fine wind-blown sand, no trace of earthworm activity, reduced rainfall and indications of a drier and windier climate. Evidence shows that skeleton-thin sheep and cattle died of drought, and up to 28,000 people abandoned the site, seeking wetter areas elsewhere. Tell Brak shrank in size by 75%. Trade collapsed. Nomadic herders such as the Amorites moved herds closer to reliable water suppliers, bringing them into conflict with Akkadian populations. This climate-induced collapse seems to have affected the whole of the Middle East, and to have coincided with the collapse of the Egyptian Old Kingdom.

This collapse of rain-fed agriculture in the Upper Country meant the loss to southern Mesopotamia of the agrarian subsidies which had kept the Akkadian Empire solvent. Water levels within the Tigris and Euphrates fell 1.5 meters beneath the level of 2600 BC, and although they stabilized for a time during the following Ur III period, rivalries between pastoralists and farmers increased. Attempts were undertaken to prevent the former from herding their flocks in agricultural lands, such as the building of a 180 km (112 mi) wall known as the "Repeller of the Amorites" between the Tigris and Euphrates under the Ur III ruler Shu-Sin. Such attempts led to increased political instability; meanwhile, severe depression occurred to re-establish demographic equilibrium with the less favorable climatic conditions.

The period between ca. 2112 BC and 2004 BC is known as the Ur III period. Documents again began to be written in Sumerian, although Sumerian was becoming a purely literary or liturgical language, much as Latin later would be in Medieval Europe.

There were a number of factors that led to the fall of the Akkadian Empire, but there were other factors at work.

CHAPTER SEVEN

BABYLONIA/EGYPT/INDIA

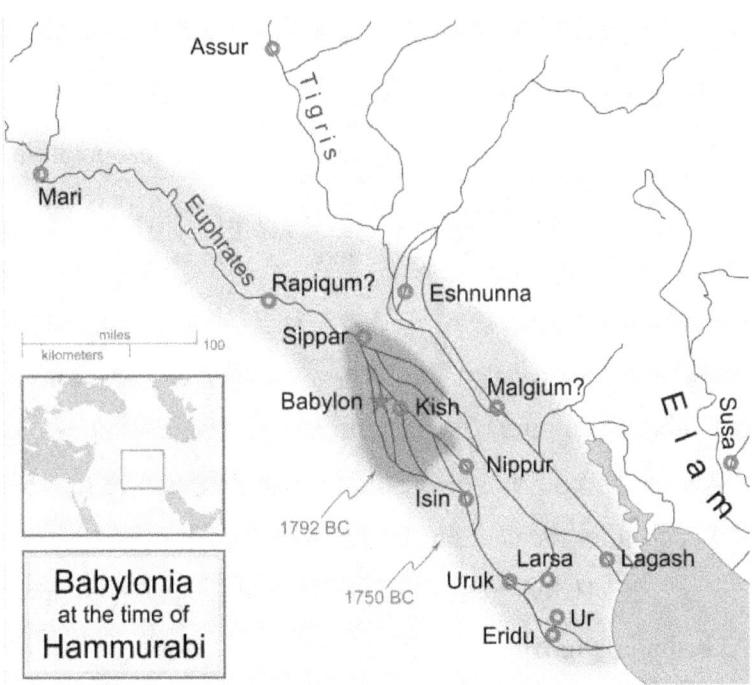

Figure 19: Babylonia during the time of Hammurabi

During this period of time there were a number of regional powers, ranging from Babylonia to Egypt and even one about which little has been written that dominated

India. Babylonia was an ancient Akkadian-speaking Semitic state and cultural region based in central-southern Mesopotamia (present-day Iraq). A small Amorite-ruled state emerged in 1894 BC, which contained at this time the minor city of Babylon. Babylon greatly expanded during the reign of Hammurabi in the first half of the 18th century BC, becoming a major capital city.

During the reign of Hammurabi and afterwards, Babylonia was called Mât Akkadî "the country of Akkad" in Akkadian. It was often involved in rivalry with its older fellow Akkadian state of Assyria in northern Mesopotamia. Babylonia briefly became the major power in the region after Hammurabi (fl. c. 1792 – 1752 BC middle chronology, or c. 1696 – 1654 BC, short chronology) created a short-lived empire, succeeding the earlier Akkadian Empire, Neo-Sumerian Empire, and Old Assyrian Empire; however, the Babylonian empire rapidly fell apart after the death of Hammurabi.

The Babylonian state retained the written Semitic Akkadian language for official use (the language of its native populace), despite its Amorite founders and Kassite successors not being native Akkadians, and speaking a Northwest Semitic Canaanite language and a Language Isolate respectively. It retained the Sumerian language for religious use (as did Assyria), but by the time Babylon was founded this was no longer a spoken language, having been wholly subsumed by Akkadian. The earlier Akkadian and Sumerian traditions played a major role in Babylonian (and Assyrian) culture, and the region would remain an important cultural center, even under protracted periods of outside rule.

The earliest mention of the city of Babylon can be found in a tablet from the reign of Sargon of Akkad (2334–2279 BC), dating back to the 23rd century BC. Babylon was merely a religious and cultural center at this point and neither an independent state nor a large city; like the rest of Mesopotamia, it was subject to the Akkadian Empire which united all the Akkadian and Sumerian speakers under one rule. After the collapse of the Akkadian empire, the south Mesopotamian region was dominated by the Gutians for a few decades before the rise of the Neo-Sumerian Empire (third dynasty of Ur), which, apart from northern Assyria, encompassed the whole of Mesopotamia, including the city of Babylon.

Of course, Babylonia had an advantage in building a strong empire and that was the remnants of the Sumerian Empire, both knowledge as well as infrastructure. In fact, the Tower of babel was actually a Sumerian ziggurat. More than buildings came from Sumeria, some of the mysterious knowledge and guidance that had led the Sumerians came as well.

All three empires firmly believed in ghosts, creatures of the night, and

It is also interesting to note that Sumeria, Akkadia and Babylonia all three grew to power in the same region of Mesopotamia. There had to be some sort of connection.

In each of these empires, there are a number of missing links and unknown that led both the rise as well as the fall of these early civilizations. Could there have been other factors at work such as extraterrestrial guidance that allowed these early powers to rise to their place in the sun before entering that final eclipse that eventually comes to all powers?

Egypt

A major player in the Middle East has long been Egypt. Ancient Egypt was a civilization of ancient Northeastern Africa, concentrated along the lower reaches of the Nile River in what is now the modern country of Egypt. It is one of six civilizations globally to arise independently. Egyptian civilization coalesced around 3150 BC (according to conventional Egyptian chronology) with the political unification of Upper and Lower Egypt under the first pharaoh. The history of ancient Egypt occurred in a series of stable Kingdoms, separated by periods of relative instability known as Intermediate Periods: the Old Kingdom of the Early Bronze Age, the Middle Kingdom of the Middle Bronze Age and the New Kingdom of the Late Bronze Age.

Egypt reached the pinnacle of its power during the New Kingdom, in the Ramesside period where it rivalled the Hittite Empire, Assyrian Empire and Mitanni Empire, after which it entered a period of slow decline. Egypt was invaded or conquered by a succession of foreign powers, such as the Canaanites/Hyksos, Libyans, the Nubians, the Assyrians, Babylonians, the Achaemenid Persians, and the Macedonians in the Third Intermediate Period and the Late Period of Egypt. In the aftermath of Alexander the Great's death, one of his generals, Ptolemy Soter, established himself as the new ruler of Egypt. This Greek Ptolemaic Dynasty ruled Egypt until 30 BC, when, under Cleopatra, it fell to the Roman Empire and became a Roman province.

The success of ancient Egyptian civilization came partly from its ability to adapt to the conditions of the Nile River valley for agriculture. The predictable flooding and controlled irrigation of the fertile valley produced surplus crops, which supported a more dense population, and social development and culture. With resources to spare, the administration sponsored mineral exploitation of the valley and surrounding desert regions, the early development of an independent writing system, the organization of collective construction and agricultural projects, trade with surrounding regions, and a military intended to defeat foreign enemies and assert Egyptian dominance. Motivating and organizing these activities was a bureaucracy of elite scribes, religious leaders, and administrators under the control of a pharaoh, who ensured the cooperation and unity of the Egyptian people in the context of an elaborate system of religious beliefs.

The many achievements of the ancient Egyptians include the quarrying, surveying and construction techniques that supported the building of monumental pyramids, temples, and obelisks; a system of mathematics, a practical and effective system of medicine, irrigation systems and agricultural production techniques, the first known ships, Egyptian faience and glass technology, new forms of literature, and the earliest known peace treaty, made with the Hittites. Egypt left a lasting legacy. Its art and architecture were widely copied, and its antiquities carried off to far corners of the world. Its monumental ruins have inspired the imaginations of travelers and writers for centuries. A new-found respect for antiquities and excavations in the early modern period by Europeans and Egyptians led to the scientific investigation of Egyptian civilization and a greater appreciation of its cultural legacy.

India

The history of India begins with evidence of human activity of anatomically modern humans, as long as 75,000 years ago, or with earlier hominids including Homo erectus from about 500,000 years ago.

The Indus Valley Civilization, which spread and flourished in the northwestern part of the Indian subcontinent from c. 3300 to 1300 BCE in present-day Pakistan and northwest India, was the first major civilization in South Asia. A sophisticated and technologically advanced urban culture developed in the Mature Harappan period, from 2600 to 1900 BCE. This civilization collapsed at the start of the second millennium BCE and was later followed by the Iron Age Vedic Civilization, which extended over much of the Indo-Gangetic plain and which witness the rise of major polities known as the Mahajanapadas. In one of these kingdoms, Magadha, Mahavira and Gautama Buddha propagated their

Shramanic philosophies during the fifth and sixth century BCE.

Most of the subcontinent was conquered by the Maurya Empire during the 4th and 3rd centuries BCE. From the 3rd century BC onwards Prakrit and Pali literature in the north and the Sangam literature in southern India started to flourish. The famous Wootz steel originated in south India in the 3rd century BC and was also exported to foreign countries.

There most common dominator of all of these ancient empires is the belief of many of its citizens that their leaders were in some fashion divine or at least semi-divine. From the leaders of Sumer to the Gilgamesh, there was a firm belief that the leaders were demi-gods, able to call of their parents, the gods for help.

Even Alexander the Great believed that his mother had been seduced by a god and as a result he was a demi-god. Even stranger there is evidence that Alexander may have been right as shown by the next section.

ALEXANDER THE GREAT

Alexander III of Macedon (20/21 July 356 – 10/11 June 323 BC), commonly known as Alexander the Great was a king of the Greek kingdom of Macedonia. Born in Pella in 356 BC, Alexander succeeded his father, Philip II to the throne at the age of twenty[43]. He spent most of his ruling years on an unprecedented military campaign through Asia and northeast Africa, until by the age of thirty he had created one of the largest empires of the ancient world, stretching from Greece to Egypt and into present-day Pakistan. He was undefeated in battle and is considered one of history's most successful commanders.

Figure 20: Bust of Alexander the Great

During his youth, Alexander was tutored by the philosopher Aristotle until the age of 16. When he succeeded his father to the throne in 336 BC, after Philip was assassinated, Alexander inherited a strong kingdom

---

[43] There were rumors that he assassinated his father to gain the throne.

and an experienced army. He had been awarded the generalship of Greece and used this authority to launch his father's military expansion plans. In 334 BC, he invaded the Achaemenid Empire, ruled Asia Minor, and began a series of campaigns that lasted ten years. Alexander broke the power of Persia in a series of decisive battles, most notably the battles of Issus and Gaugamela. He subsequently overthrew the Persian King Darius III and conquered the entirety of the Persian Empire. At that point, his empire stretched from the Adriatic Sea to the Indus River.

Figure 21: Philip of Macedonia

Seeking to reach the "ends of the world and the Great Outer Sea", he invaded India in 326 BC, but was eventually forced to turn back at the demand of his troops. Alexander died in Babylon in 323 BC, the city he planned to establish as his capital, without executing a series of planned campaigns that would have begun with an invasion of Arabia. In the years following his death, a series of civil wars tore his empire apart, resulting in several states ruled by the Diadochi, (Alexander's surviving generals and heirs).

Figure 22: Alexander the Great in Battle

While it was not well known there are several instances when UFOs seemed to favor Alexander's efforts in battle. The first recorded incident regarding Alexander the Great and UFO's was recorded in 329 BC[44].

Alexander decided to invade India and was attempting to cross the river Indus to engage the Indian army when "gleaming silver shields" swooped down and made several passes over the battle. These "gleaming silver shields" had the effect of startling his cavalry horses, causing them to stampede. They also had a similar effect on

---

[44] Drake, W. Raymond, 'Gods and Spacemen in Greece and Rome', Sphere, London 1976, pp. 115-116:

the enemies' horses and elephants so it was difficult to ascertain whose side these "gleaming silver shields" were on. Nevertheless, after exiting the battle victoriously Alexander decided to not proceed any further into India.

Seven years later, in 332 B C, Alexander was confronted with the greatest challenge of his military career. In his attempt to conquer the Persian Empire he realized that the city of Tyre needed to be captured in order to prevent the Persians from using that port to land an army behind him. The original coastal city of Tyre had been destroyed before and had been rebuilt some distance offshore from its original site[45].

Figure 23: Ancient City of Tyre

---

[45] Alberto Fenoglio, "Cronistoria su oggetti volanti del passato, - Appunti per una clipeostoria", 'Clypeus' #9, 1st Semester 1966, p. 7

Having no navy, Alexander decided to use the remains of the old city to build a causeway to the new one. It took Alexander six full months to do this and when the task was completed and his troops staged their assault they were easily rebuffed because the walls were too high to quickly scale and too thick to batter down. Not only was the wall too high and too thick, but the causeway was too narrow to allow sufficient troops to launch a massive enough attack to overwhelm the enemy in order to scale the walls.

Not only was this a problem for Alexander but apparently a problem for God as well. Both the prophets Ezekiel and Isaiah had spoken of Gods' curse and eventual destruction of Tyre[46]. How was Alexander going to achieve his goal? How was God going to ensure that His prophecy would be fulfilled?

The historical account, recorded by Alexander's chief historian, states that, during an attack of the island city, one of two 'gleaming silver shields' attacked a section of the wall with a 'beam of light' which subsequently caused that section of the wall to fall! Alexander's' men poured through the opening and captured the city[47].

---

[46] Ezekiel Chapters 27 & 28 and Isaiah Chapter 23
[47] Quoting Giovanni Gustavo Droysens Storia di Alessandro il Grande, Alberto Fenoglio, writes in CLYPEUS Anno 111, No 2

Once again it would seem that mysterious forces took a direct hand in a war between different groups of humans. This is definite proof of alien intervention in the affairs of men.

CHAPTER EIGHT

ENCOUNTERS BETWEEN GODS AND HUMANS

Close Encounters

In UFO jargon there are several types of contacts as shown below:

- Close Encounters of the First Kind are simply UFO sightings.
- Close Encounters of the Second Kind are sightings of UFOs accompanied by the physical evidence of an alien craft.
- Close Encounters of the Third Kind are those in which a human has contact with the intelligent beings inside the craft.
- Close Encounters of the Fourth Kind are human abductions by aliens

- Close Encounters of the Fifth Kind are encounters of a more intimate nature.

We have looked at the issue of contact between the "gods" and men on a national scale, but what about contact between "gods" and individuals? Now we come to the crux of the issue at hand. Have so-called gods, or perhaps we should say Annunaki had their way with human females? We know that Annunaki helped to impart advanced knowledge to the leaders of the early civilizations, but did Annunaki involvement with humans go even further?

A review of numerous allegations of alien contact and abduction it becomes clear that these "visitors" have a very deep interest in human anatomy as well as sexual reproduction. A review of some historic incidents, viewed as myth up to now, would tend to show why this might be.

Zeus, King of the Gods

Figure 24: Zeus, King of the Gods

A major factor in the well-known tragedies surrounding Heracles is the hatred that the goddess Hera, wife of Zeus, had for him. A full account of Heracles must render it clear why Heracles was so tormented by Hera, when there were many illegitimate offspring sired by Zeus. Heracles was the son of the affair Zeus had with the mortal woman Alcmene. Zeus made love to her after disguising himself as her husband, Amphitryon, home early from war (Amphitryon did return later the same night, and Alcmene became pregnant with his son at the same time, a case of heteropaternal superfecundation, where a woman carries twins sired by different fathers). Thus, Heracles' very existence proved at least one of Zeus' many illicit affairs, and Hera often conspired against Zeus' mortal offspring as revenge for her husband's infidelities. His twin mortal brother, son of Amphitryon, was Iphicles, father of Heracles' charioteer Iolaus.

On the night the twins Heracles and Iphicles were to be born, Hera, knowing of her husband Zeus' adultery, persuaded Zeus to swear an oath that the child born that night to a member of the House of Perseus would become High King. Hera did this knowing that while Heracles was to be born a descendant of Perseus, so too was Eurystheus. Once the oath was sworn, Hera hurried to Alcmene's dwelling and slowed the birth of the twins Heracles and Iphicles by forcing Ilithyia, goddess of childbirth, to sit cross-legged with her clothing tied in knots, thereby causing the twins to be trapped in the womb. Meanwhile, Hera caused Eurystheus to be born prematurely, making him High King in place of Heracles. She would have permanently delayed Heracles' birth had she not been fooled by Galanthis, Alcmene's servant, who lied to Ilithyia, saying that Alcmene had already delivered the baby. Upon hearing this, she jumped in surprise, loosening the knots and inadvertently allowing Alcmene to give birth to Heracles and Iphicles.

This is one of the earliest instances of the gods becoming involved in the affairs of man and of a god seducing a human female but as we shall see it was not the only one.

Boys Will Be Boys, Even Alien Boys

For hundreds, perhaps thousands of years, there have been stories of human females being abducted and in many cases forced to engage in sexual relations with unknown entities. Carl Sagan told the story of Anne Jefferies, a Cornish teenager in 1645.

Anne was the victim of an alien visitation. Not being familiar with such terms as UFOs or flying saucers, when Anne was found groggy and crumpled on the floor, she told a story of being attacked by little men, carried paralyzed to a castle in the air, seduced and then returned home. She referred to those little men that kidnapped her as fairies. Unfortunately, she lived in a time when the Devil was responsible for everything so instead of investigating her story, she was arrested for witchcraft.

South American Fun in the Sun

Figure 25: Landing flying saucer

We have all heard about the story of Betty and Barney Hill in 1961, however, four years before that was a most unusual event that took place in Brazil. From this Brazilian event it became clear that certain mysterious entities were engaged in a program of interbreeding that involved the human race.

Antonio Villas Boas was a 23 year old law student who worked on his family's farm to earn the money to pay his way through school. Like many famers of the time, he preferred to work in the late afternoon evening to avoid the hot temperatures of the day. On October 16, 1957, he was ploughing fields near São Francisco de Sales when he saw what he described as a "red star" in the night sky. According to his story, this "star" approached his position, growing in size until it became recognizable as a roughly circular or egg-shaped aerial craft, with a red light at its front and a rotating cupola on top. The craft began descending to land in the field, extending three "legs" as it did so. At that point, Boas decided to run from the scene.

  According to Boas, he first attempted to leave the scene on his tractor, but when its lights and engine died after traveling only a short distance, he decided to continue on foot. However, he was seized by a 1.5 m (five-foot) tall humanoid, who was wearing grey coveralls and a helmet. Its eyes were small and blue, and instead of speech it made noises like barks or yelps. Three similar beings then joined the first in subduing Boas, and they dragged him inside their craft.

Figure 26: Naked female alien

Once inside the craft, Boas said that he was stripped of his clothes and covered from head-to-toe with a strange gel. He was then led into a large semicircular room, through a doorway that had strange red symbols written over it. (Boas claimed that he was able to memorize these symbols and later reproduced them for investigators.) In this room the beings took samples of Boas' blood from his chin. After this he was then taken to a third room and left alone for around half an hour. During this time, some kind of gas was pumped into the room, which made Boas become violently ill.

Figure 27: Antonio Villas-Boas

Shortly after this, Boas claimed that he was joined in the room by another humanoid. This one, however, was female, very attractive, and naked. She was the same height as the other beings he had encountered, with a small, pointed chin and large, blue catlike eyes. The hair on her head was long and white (somewhat like platinum blonde) but her underarm and pubic hair was bright red. Boas said he was strongly attracted to the woman, and the two had sexual intercourse. During this act, Boas noted that the female did not kiss him but instead nipped him on the chin.

When it was all over, the female smiled at Boas, rubbing her belly and gestured upwards. Boas took this to mean that she was going to raise their child in space. The female seemed relieved that their "task" was over, and Boas himself said that he felt angered by the situation, because he felt as though he had been little more than "a good stallion" for the humanoids.

Boas said that he was then given back his clothing and taken on a tour of the ship by the humanoids. During this tour he said that he attempted to take a clock-like device as proof of his encounter, but was caught by the humanoids and prevented from doing so. He was then escorted off the ship and watched as it took off, glowing brightly. When Boas returned home, he discovered that four hours had passed. Unfortunately, few originally believed his story though he stuck by it until his death in 1991[48].

Kidnapped From Her Bed

Figure 28: Alien grey - bedroom visitation

Another victim of Alien visitation was a young lady by the name of Jane Murphy. Up until one night in 1981, Jane, a resident of Birstall, West Yorkshire, led a very normal life. But on this night all that changed. She dropped into bed, exhausted expecting to wake up to the same life she had when she went to sleep, but this was not destined to be.

A few hours later, she woke up to a strange world. She was immediately aware that something was wrong so she did not open her eyes. She listened carefully but did not

---

[48] http://theunexplainedmysteries.com/Antonio-Villas-Boas-Alien-Abduction.html

hear her husband's comforting snores. She also had the distinct impression that something was wrong with the room. Instead of the normal sounds of her bedroom she heard only the sounds of the night as if she was outside.

Figure 29: Levitated from her bed

Finally, unable to control her curiosity, Jane opened her eyes to see that she was lying on the ground in a field near her mother's house. She had no idea how she had arrived at this location.

She tried to get to her feet, but saw a group of humanoid figures approaching her. She tried to get away but one of them forced a cloth over her face and she passed out. The last thing she was aware of was an injection in her thigh.

When Jane next was aware of anything she was in a strange room, surrounded by alien looking creatures. Most of them were small creatures but one of them was at least seven feet tall though he looked like a normal human male, though his eyes were totally black.

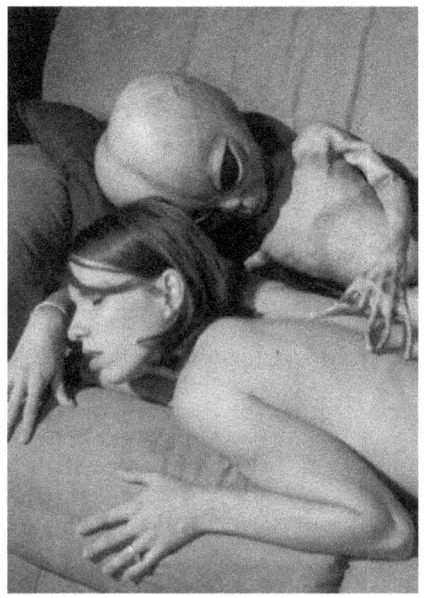

Figure 30: Alien male/human female

As she sat upon on the edge of the examination table wearing only her somewhat revealing nightgown, a young seeming alien woman approached her and said that she must take a bath. Surprisingly, Jane found herself obeying the instructions. She slipped off her night gown and got into a tub that seemed to accommodate itself to her form. Slowly, almost sensuously, Jane bathed her body from head to toe before stepping from the tub to stand naked in the middle of the room. She saw that all of the aliens had left except for the big one.

Reaching out for her, the tall alien led Jane over to a table located in the middle of the room. Jane remembered that she just stared into his big, black eyes, unresisting, knowing what was going to happen to her. She was never sure if he had raped her or simply seduced her. Whatever may have been the cause, she discovered that she had no thought of resisting whatever he wanted to do to her. In fact when he lay back on the table, without any urging, she climbed on top of him wanting him to make love to her.

Although they embraced, she remembered that there was very little movement and she was not even aware of him penetrating her. She had no thoughts of the physical act, but nevertheless felt all of the sensations of normal human sex. She later said that inside her it was all happening. In fact, she described it as the best sex she had ever had. It seemed so strange to her, lying on top of this stranger, not moving yet having sex and enjoying it. If anything, the only thing that caused her discomfort was his strange, inhuman smell.

Figure 31: Almost every abduction ends with a gynecological exam

At one point, Jane looked deep into his eyes and said *"why are you doing this to me?"* He responded telepathically, *"Because we love you."* Though he had used the word love, she knew that it was no real emotion behind his words. Clearly he was cold and emotionless. In spite of this, she said she climaxed and realized that this was the best sex she had ever had.

After she had climaxed, the alien set up and moved her to a position beside the table. The other aliens, including several females took charge of her while her sexual partner got off the table and left the room. At this point she was given a gynecological examination with a long instrument, though she said she felt no pain during this examination.

After the conclusion of her exam, Jane was taken on a tour of the ship and then given some pills and a liquid refreshment. Suddenly, she found that she was back in her own bed, it was 6:30 A.M. and her alarm clock was going off. She was relieved to find that her night time adventures had all been a dream. This feeling of relief was not to last.

After a few minutes of being awake, she noticed a peculiar, inhuman odor which sent her off to the bathroom for a long bath. While in the bath, she discovered some mysterious puncture marks on her body. She realized that these mysterious punctures were exactly where the aliens had injected her. Then she began to feel a distinctive feeling in the pit of her stomach which she remembered being associated with her bring pregnant. When her period was late, she was frightened. She was now sure that her memories of the event were real memories of an actual event that had happened to her and not distant memories of a dream.

Jane's next move was to go to the doctor for an examination. The doctor assured her that she was not pregnant but she did have a very unusual vaginal infection which after a period of time was eventually cleared up with a course of very powerful antibiotics. With a feeling of relief, Jane thought her unusual experience was at an end; unfortunately this was not to be.

Within a month, Jane awoke to find the aliens standing around her bed. They swarmed all over the house and bombarded her with questions about human reproduction. Although she had no clear memories of being abducted once against, she had the very distinct feeling that this had occurred, possibly more than once.

Soon she was having dreams in which she gave birth to a blond, black-eyed, alien baby. At this point she decided that she was going out of her mind, there was no doubt that she was heading for nervous breakdown. Her doctor suspected that she was taking illegal drugs and although her husband professed not to believe her stories of great sex with an alien, it was having a decided negative impact on their marriage.

Not knowing what to do next, Jane finally contacted the British UFO Research Association's[49] hot line. Under their examination it was discovered that she had been abducted several times and that she had very likely given

---

[49] BUFORA is a non-cultist and scientifically evaluative organization since its formation in 1962, when a number of UFO research organizations and individuals formed with an inaugural meeting at Kensington, London.

These included societies such as the British Flying Saucer Bureau and the London UFO Research organization, early magazine producers and individual investigators. The BUFORA Journal was produced from 1962 and under various titles, was the mainstay of contact for members until the website took over exclusively in 2005. A magazine format may return in the future.

Hundreds of cases have been published in the journal and special study booklets have been produced in over half a century of ongoing focus on all aspects of the UFO phenomenon. The complete collection of all of these can be purchased on one single DVD at the BUFORA products section of this site.

Conferences have been staged since the 1960s at regular frequencies, with our fiftieth anniversary staged in London in 2012. BUFORA continues to be a major contributor and consultant to news, documentaries and articles over the decades, with many prominent UFO authors as part of its team throughout its history.

Since the 1970s, the association has run a specialist training course in investigations. BUFORA also formed a code of practice for investigators which continues into the present, with all reports lead by the witness in every case.

Special studies include ongoing data collection, such as the Anamnesis project and Vehicle Interference Reports. BUFORA adopts an open and analytical view to all cases and report categories and continues to explore the UFO phenomena with an open mind, with no belief systems or exclusive theories in its continuing investigations.

An excellent introduction to the UFO subject can be found on the tab: "Guide to UFOs"

birth to an alien baby which was taken from her by the aliens.

Though this is a very unusual story, it is no different from the so-called myths regarding Zeus coming down to Earth to seduce the mother of Hercules. If the aliens can control the minds of their selected mates to induce sexual passion, then how many times has this happened to women who do not remember all of the details?[50]

Another Tale of a Sexual Encounter

Figure 32: Taken by Surprise

Lest the reader think that Jane's story was a one-time event, let us turn our attention to another encounter researched by BUFORA[51]. This particular lady was from Taunton in Somerset, married and by all accounts happy with her life.

---

[50] http://bufora.org.uk/ BUFORA Journal, Digital Archive Collection 1959-2005.
[51] British UFO Research Association

Figure 33: Alien with big black emotionless eyes

On the night in question, she was driving near her home when suddenly the engine of her car quit. Coasting over to the side of the road, she left her car to look under the hood to try and determine what was wrong with her car. As she bent over the motor, she was grabbed from behind, which was the last thing she remembered for some time.

When she regained consciousness, she found that she was no longer alongside the road, but she was now naked, tied to a table of some sort and covered with a blanket. There were three aliens wearing blue outfits thoroughly examining her naked body. Each of these creatures was around 5'6" in height, fair skins having large round, emotionless eyes. Two of the aliens eventually left the room and the third one gave her an injection in the thigh which left her body somewhat numb.

Once she was somewhat out of it from the injection, the third alien undressed and crawled on top of her. Coldly and with little signed of emotion, she brutally raped her helpless body until she passed out. When she awoke, she found that she was dressed and once again beside her car which now worked perfectly. Some little time had passed and when she arrived home, her husband was beginning a search for her. Both the BUFORA investigator and her husband found her story credible. Something definitely had happened to her alongside that road. However, in this case there were no reports of a pregnancy, but medical examination did show that she had been involved in intercourse.

A Recap

It is interesting to note that though this domination of humans by aliens has gone on for thousands of years, the alien abductors still insist on giving thorough exams to those they take. It would make it appear that perhaps we are dealing with some type of long running breeding program.

There is no doubt that the abductors see no problem with taking sexual advantage of their captives. There are hundreds of stories going back thousands of years about these entities, whether they are called demons, aliens or any other type of paranormal creature raping human females. So let us go further into an examination of the activities of these nocturnal rapists.

Figure 34: The last sight many abductees see

CHAPTER NINE
BIBLICAL ENCOUNTERS

From no less a source than the Christian Holy Bible there are numerous tales of encounters between "gods" and man. Though mainstream religion believes that each of these encounters was with the one true God, there are some questions that have troubled researchers over the years.

There are a number of paranormal events in both the Old as well as the New Testament. Of course, the conservative Christian movement has found much to criticize about the very idea of giving a paranormal meaning to some of the events in the Bible. However, if one is not afraid to delve deeply into the various books of the Bible, a completely new story emerges. We also find the main thrust of this book throughout the Bible, once the religious trapping are removed, we find a continual thread of the fascination with sexual activity and conception by and between Humans and Aliens.

Though traditional biblical scholars have long regard psychic interpretations of the Bible as mythological or even demonic, or perhaps merely symbolic or metaphorical, such a view does give one pause to think. Between the Book of Genesis and the Book of Revelations there are stories of:

- alien visitation to Earth,
- angels,
- mediums,
- psychics
- soothsayers,
- astrologers,
- numerology,
- witches and wizards,
- dreams,
- divination,
- healings,
- apparitions,
- visions,
- astral travel,
- psychokinesis,
- clairvoyance,

- telepathy,
- precognition,
- premonitions,
- prophecies and of course
- the paranormal gifts and miracles attributed to both Moses as well as Jesus.

Figure 35: Moses and the Burning Bush

One of the major miracles in the Bible is the story of Moses encountering the burning bush. Out of that burning bush which was not consumed, came the voice of God who sent Moses to free the Hebrews and lead them to the Promised Land. Whether it was the Voice of God or that of what we might call an Annunaki, this event changed the course of the world as it was known at the time. Any activity that was not done by human hands could be said to be alien activity. This intervention by forces beyond our understanding changed the balance of power in that part of the world and eventually across the world.

Moses was certain it was the voice of God as a bush that burned without being consumed was considered magic in his time and place. However, remember Clark's Third Law[52]: *Any sufficiently advanced technology is indistinguishable from magic.* It can be argued that the burning bush was the result of some advanced form of technology. We could do the same thing today with lasers and holograms. Does this mean that it was not God speaking from the burning bush?

There have been many instances when aliens have told human contactees that it as the aliens that created religion as a control mechanism. Certainly religion has long proved to be a greater motivator and control mechanism than secular government. In *The Occult Connection: UFOs,*

---

[52] Clarke's Three Laws are three "laws" of prediction formulated by the British science fiction writer Arthur C. Clarke. They are:
1. When a distinguished but elderly scientist states that something is possible, he is almost certainly right. When he states that something is impossible, he is very probably wrong.
2. The only way of discovering the limits of the possible is to venture a little way past them into the impossible.
3. Any sufficiently advanced technology is indistinguishable from magic.

Secret Societies and Ancient Gods[53], I go into a thorough discussion of this question backed up by a number of sources that make it clear that even if the aliens did not create our regions, they certainly used them to their benefit.

Angels

Figure 36: Angels are normally depicted with wings

Throughout the Bible there are discussions of angels, said to be God's messengers. In fact it was said to be a war in Heaven, a rebellion of some of the Angels that led to the introduction of evil on the Earth through the ministrations of Satan. Another Angel is said to be the Arch

---

[53] Hudnall, Ken, *UFOs, Secret Societies and Ancient Gods*, Omega Press, 1989.

Angel Michael, called by many God's Mercenary. He is almost always depicted with a weapon. In fact it was said to be Michael that actually cast Satan out of Heaven.

Figure 37: A depiction of Michael, said to be God's Mercenary

There are questions as to whether God or one of the Angels actually dictated the Ten Commandments to Moses as there is no evidence that Moses had anything to do with the creation of these rules which were meant to control the population.

But in keeping with our premise that the "visitors" had an unusual interest in the sexual activity of humans we need look no further than Hagar, servant of Abraham.

Figure 38: Abraham, Sarah and Isaac

If you will recall, Abraham's wife, Sarah, was unable to bear him any children, so he made Hagar, their servant pregnant. Sarah became angry and punished Hagar. Hagar ran away. The "Angel of the Lord" appeared to Hagar and told her to return to Abraham's tent and that she would bear a son by the name of Ishmael. Abraham was 86 when his son Ishmael was born. Ishmael became the father of the Arab peoples.

However, this was not the end of the involvement of the involvement of angels with Abraham and his family.

When Abraham and Sarah were both past the age of ninety, a trio of angels appeared to them and told them that they would have a son whose name would be Isaac. It also seems somewhat odd that God would take the time to name two individuals before their birth. What did this accomplish? Apparently it was a part of some master plan.

It would seem most likely that with Abraham over ninety and Sarah having not shown any signs of being fertile up to this point that we are most likely dealing with a case of artificial insemination. Why was it necessary that Abraham and Sarah have a child at this late date in their lives?

Figure 39: The virgin birth of Jesus

In the case of the birth of Jesus, it was an angel that came to tell Mary that she would give birth to Jesus. She was, according to the scripture to have a virgin birth. The virgin birth of Jesus is the belief that Jesus was conceived in the womb of his mother Mary through the Holy Spirit without the agency of a human father and born while Mary was yet a virgin. The New Testament references are Matthew 1:18-25 and Luke 1:26-38. It is not expressly mentioned elsewhere in the Christian scriptures, and "the modern scholarly consensus is that the doctrine of the virgin birth rests on a very slim historical foundation."

The virgin birth was universally accepted in the Christian church by the 2nd century and, except for some minor sects, was not seriously challenged until the 18th century. It is enshrined in the creeds that most Christians consider normative, such as the Nicene Creed ("incarnate of the Virgin Mary") and the Apostles' Creed ("born of the Virgin Mary"), and is a basic article of belief in the Roman Catholic, Orthodox, and most Protestant churches. Muslims also accept the virgin birth of Jesus.

Assuming that there is some truth to the concept of the virgin birth, then it is very likely that the "conceiving of Jesus in the womb of the mother by the Holy Spirit referred to artificial insemination of a situation similar to that of

Jane Murphy. There is little doubt that throughout history, sex has been used as both an award as well as a way to control and change the human race.

An Unhealthy Interest

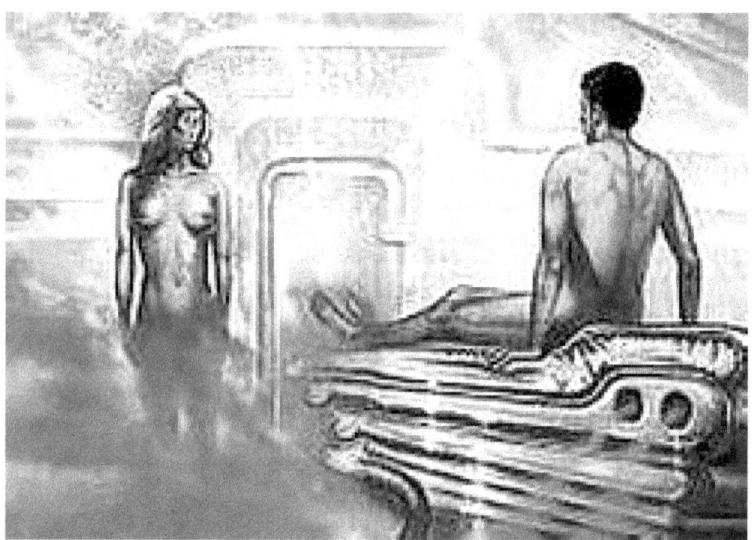

Figure 40: She had no control over her body

There is no doubt that since the earliest days of this planet those we now call aliens have had a somewhat unhealthy interest in sexual relations between humans, using it as a method of influencing bloodlines and shifting entire dynasties through sexual relations.

But it also seems that the aliens don't just want to have sex with humans, they like to also watch humans making love and they have an abiding interest in human reproduction.

David M. Jacobs of Temple University reported that a young woman was abducted in 1988 and forced to have sex with an unconscious man. During an interview, she later recalled that she was made to climb on top of the comatose man[54].

According to the young lady in question, she was sitting straddling the unconscious man and one of the aliens told her, telepathically to kiss him. She did not want to do so, so she put her hand on his chest and pretended to the aliens that this was a human kiss. They seemed to believe her explanation which raises some interesting questions.

The aliens next instructed her to touch the man's penis. She was ordered to scoot down the man's body. She responded that she didn't want to have oral sex with him and tried to convince the aliens not to force her to do this. They did not physically force her, but she stated that their will was very strong.

The aliens next instructed her to have sex with the unconscious man and to her shock, under their control, his penis became erect. She tried her best to resist their orders, but she found herself having sex with the man. She

---

[54] BUFORA Journal, Digital Archive Collection 1959-2005.

described it as being mechanical without any emotion on her part. She was literally their mindless puppet.

Figure 41: Physical exam by aliens

The woman reported that after the two had finished having sex, her mind went blank as if they had simply turned her off. When she was next aware, she found that she was now sexually aroused. Luckily for her the man had remained erect.

Eventually she was returned by her captors. She never saw the man again and she was relieved to find that she was not pregnant. It seemed to be an experiment by the aliens into human sexuality. If this is taking place I our advanced technological society, how many times did such activity take place in the remote past and how did these encounters effect early civilization?

Female aliens Need Sex Too

It should be noted that it is not just alien males that abuse female humans, but there are female aliens who seem to need sex as well. On September 28, 1985, a man by the name of Ted Johnson was driving on a deserted road in Essex when he saw a strange light in the distance[55]. Thinking it might be someone in trouble, he pulled over to the side of the road and left his car to try and determine what he had seen.

Figure 42: From the description of the light

Shortly after leaving his car, Ted heard a low whistling sound and the light came so close to him that it hurt his eyes. After a few seconds there was a green flash which knocked Td to the ground and partially blinded him.

---

[55] Ibid

When he struggled back to his feet, he saw a strangely dressed female standing before him.

In form she was very attractive though her eyes were round and her nose was small. Instead of a human mouth, she had a slit and she was glowing. Behind her Johnson saw several other humanoid figures, but his eyes were all for the female alien, she seemed to have some sort of control over his mind.

Taking his hand, the female alien led Johnson to her nearby ship and into a small room. Once the door closed behind them, she stripped off her clothing and stood before him naked.

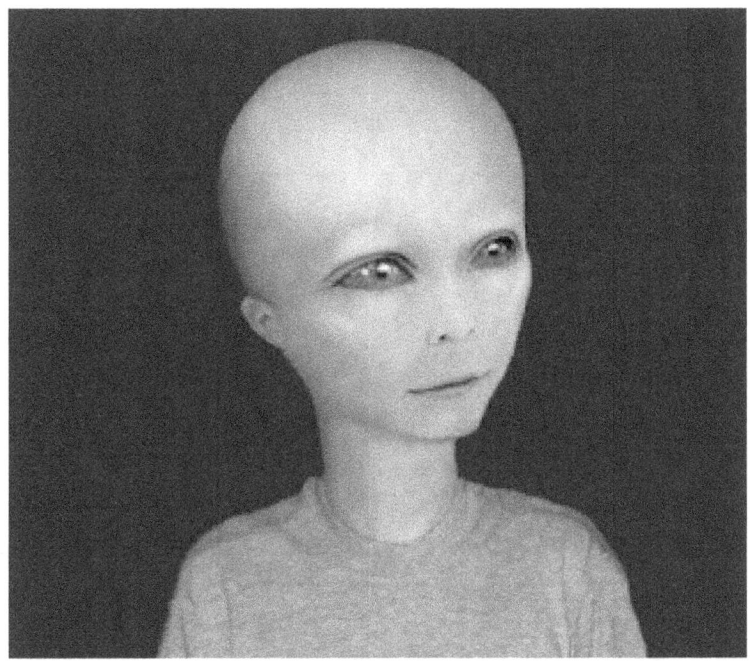

Figure 43: Human/Alien hybrid?

Johnson could never explain why he was so overcome with lust, but he had eyes for nothing but the female form before him. They had what he described as wild sex no different form human sex.

There is little doubt that there is some sort of interbreeding program going on involving the human race. The sexual encounters initiated by alien females may be in order to breed a new race of either human or aliens. When male aliens force sex on human females it may be simply for enjoyment or to create half breeds which are later removed from the care of their mothers and raised by the aliens. It is certainly interesting to note that according the encounters it is possible for humans and the aliens to interbreed.

CHAPTER TEN

MORE EVIDENCE OF INTERACTION

Figure 44: Interesting sight to wake up to

If aliens are, for lack of a better term, raping humans, then why are there not more reports? Well it appears that in some cases, the aliens are able to affect the minds of the victims so that they do not remember what happened. We must therefore, find out about these events through investigation and looking at the evidence.

So what evidence exists supporting alien abductions of humans for breeding purposes? Well sometimes when abductions are performed the aliens leave evidence behind them. Unless the victim is permanently removed, there is always the chance that he or she talks about what happened to them. Such was the case with this witness.

On the night of October 7, 1955, in the state of Nebraska, a young woman by the name of Jennie was sleeping peacefully in her bed. As she slept, something very strange happened. Though she clearly experienced something very much out of the ordinary, it was to be almost thirty years until she was fully aware of what happened[56].

In 1984, she underwent hypnotic regression and the memories were retrieved. While under hypnosis she recalled being visited by an alien creature that she referred to as the Explorer. Her first memories were of him hovering outside her bedroom window, telepathically ordering her to come to him. She said

Figure 45: Medical exam

---

[56] BUFORA Journal, Digital Archive Collection 1959-2005

Sensual Alien Encounters /127

that she tried to resist his commands, pretending she was dreaming. Unfortunately, for her, the power of his mental suggestion was too much for her to resist. She eventually asked him how she could follow him.

The Explorer informed her that she wanted to take her to his laboratory which she described as being like two dessert bowls stuck together. She reported that while she had trouble envisioning his description, he put the picture of what he was describing into her mind.

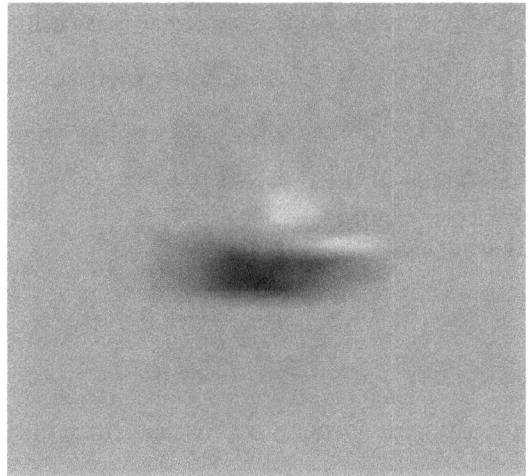

Figure 46: Hovering, fading UFO

By this point, Jennie reported that her resistance to his influence was weakening and she found that she was floating above her bed. Slowly, she found that she was floating toward him, but she knew she was safe since the window was still closed. Then to her shock, she found that she was floating through the wall, she even remembered seeing the dust and spider webs in the space between the inner and outer walls.

Once she found herself outside the house, she immediately saw the UFO hovering outside though she found that her vision was fluctuating. Finally, as she floated closer she found that the craft was fading away to the point that she could see the parking lot over which the craft hovered.

Figure 47: The Explorer studied her body thoroughly

Jennie found that the inside of the craft was even colder than the outside. She reported that it felt like she had entered a freezer. Waiting for her was the one she referred to as the Explorer. Now he was wearing a white, surgeon's cap. Assisting him were a number of smaller creatures. She described the Explorer as being between 3 and 4r feet tall with a head shaped like an egg. His face was waxy and greyish his nose was only a tiny bump with two slits and his mouth was another slit. His attitude could only be described as stern.

Jennie remembered that there was little interaction between her and her captors, with the Explorer putting information into her head telepathically as he worked. He instructed her to get up on the silver table that dominated the room. She asked where him where they were going and he responded nowhere.

Figure 48: Abductee being floated onto UFO

As soon as she was completely on the table, she was grabbed by clamps that came from the table and pulled flat on her back on the table. She found that she was helpless, completely unable to escape the claws that help her.

As she lay helpless before their eyes, her body spread eagled and bound on the silver table Jennie reported that the Explorer and an assistant began to take samples of her hair. The using a capillary tube, blood samples were taken. Jennie reported that at this point she protested that what they were doing was painful to her, but the aliens showed no signs that they particularly cared about her comfort.

After she was given a thorough exam and numerous samples were taken by her captors, she found that she was back in her bed, apparently none the worse for wear. The next morning, she found that the giant elm tree outside her window was burned. Her father told her that it had been hit by lightning the previous night, though she was sure it had something to do with her alien visitor.

Mysterious Pregnancy

Jennie did not report any further effects from her abduction, but that was not always the case. We next will look at the case of Shane Kurz, a 19 year old woman who was a nurse's assistant and who also underwent some very bizarre symptoms[57].

Figure 49: Hanz Holzer

On the night of May 3, 1968, like Jennie, Shane had gone to bed just as she did every night. Nothing out of the ordinary happened until bright lights outside caused her to look out her window about 4:00 AM. She later recalled that she saw a UFO but she remembered nothing else until her mother woke her up the

---

[57] Ibid

next morning. This was when the mystery began to get serious. She found muddy footprints that seemed to come out of the wall and walked over to surround her bed. Later, she found where the prints began outside and seemed to walk through the wall into her bedroom.

Figure 50: Alien Abductions

It was not until 1974 that she approached Professor Hanz Holzer[58], a world famous parapsychologist. Though she had no memory of what happened that night, Shane reported having suffered nightmares and migraines and been afflicted with strange red rings that appeared on her abdomen. She also reported that she stopped menstruating for over a year. The doctors she consulted were unable to find any explanation for what was happening to her. These symptoms seemed to fade away in 1973, but she was still

---

[58] Better known as a ghost hunter. He and his former wife Sybil Leek, a medium, wrote a number of books on ghosts around the world.

concerned as to what had happened to her. She felt that her symptoms had something to do with the UFO she had seen and the muddy footprints that had surrounded her bed.

Hans Holzer placed her under hypnosis and explored her memories of that night. Under hypnosis she remembered being abducted from her bedroom by aliens who seemed to walk out of the wall to surround her bed.

From Shane's description the aliens were small, with grey skins, probing eyes and none of them had any hair. Like Jennie, they took her into a large room that was dominated by the large silver table. She was placed on the table and was immobilized.

One of the aliens acted very familiar to her as if he had known her before. He stuck a long needle into her abdomen and took samples of her ova. He then told her that she had been chosen to produce a baby for them and they were conducting an examination on her to see if she was fertile. Once the exam was complete, the leader of the aliens crawled on top of her helpless body and raped her. The red rings that appeared later on her abdomen were the results of her pregnancy. The symptoms went away when the fetus was recovered from her during the night.

Female Aliens and Male Humans

While most of the stores deal with aliens impregnating female humans, there are also stories of female aliens having sex with human males.

In June 1994, while working at the Red Flag logging camp in the northwest portion of Wuchang, Meng Zhaoguo and two coworkers claimed that they had seen a strange metallic shine coming from Mount Phoenix. Meng had thought a helicopter had crashed at the location of the shine. So he set off towards the site, and as he approached what he thought was a wreck, he claimed that something hit him square in the forehead and knocked him out.

A few nights later, Meng claimed that at his house, he encountered a female alien with braided fur on her legs: He claimed that she was 10 feet (3.0 m) [3.03 meters] tall and had six fingers, but otherwise she looked completely like a human.

At the time of the encounter, he said he was floating above his bed and could see his wife and daughter below him. He said that for 40 minutes, he had sexual intercourse with the female alien. When they had finished, the female alien left the room, leaving Meng with a 5 cm mark on his thigh. A month later, he said he was levitated through a wall into a spaceship where he encountered some aliens. He asked if he could see the female alien he had been with a month earlier. They responded by telling him that it was not possible. Instead they told him that in 60 years, on a distant planet, the son of a Chinese peasant will be born. They noted that he would get a chance to see his son.

In September 2003, Meng was checked by a doctor, tested on a lie detector (which he passed), and placed under hypnosis in an attempt to reveal whether or not he had lied about the incident. Zhang Jingping, who helped initiate the testing, said that Meng's test results showed that he had told the truth about his incident. Zhang also said that after a doctor had checked Meng's scar, they had come to the conclusion that the scar "could not possibly have been caused by common injuries or surgery."

So the evidence points to very real interactions between aliens and humans. As we will see in the nexct chapter, the description of the female alien encountered by Meng matches a race that once populated this world during pre-history.

CHAPTER ELEVEN

ALIEN DESCRIPTIONS

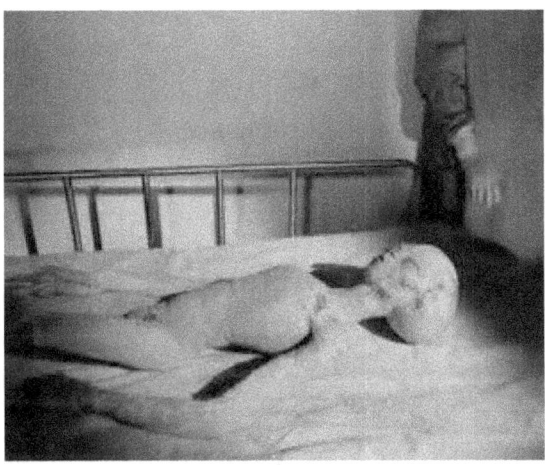

Figure 51: Dead alien?

Most of the descriptions of aliens that come out of abductions are of the so called greys, but there are descriptions of other creatures that have also been reported. For example, from the Meng Zhaoguo Incident the female alien was described as a ten-foot tall female alien with large eyes, six fingers and braided leg fur wearing a seamless rubber suit. This was followed by Meng's strangest claim of all: that the two had sex for forty minutes while floating over the bodies of his sleeping wife and daughter. The alien left a five-centimeter scar on his thigh, because she was clearly a kinky sort of gal.

Only a month later Meng was abducted again, taken aboard a pristine white spaceship filled with similar beings. He asked to see his sex pal again, but was told that it would be impossible. On the upside, his son would be born sixty years later on a distant planet.

While alien abduction stories are always taken with a grain of salt, Meng's tale raised a few eyebrows because of the relatively unique description of his abductors (braided leg fur?). However, he maintains that it really happened, and in 2003 a lie detector test and hypnosis determined that he at least believed his story. A doctor also looked into that thigh scar and determined that it couldn't have been made through common injury or surgery, lending a little more creepy credence to the story.

The Allagash Abductions

Then there are the aliens from what was called the Allagash Abductions. In 1976, four men – brothers Jack and Jim Weiner, Chuck Rak and Charlie Foltz – went on a camping trip in the woods of Allagash, Maine.

While things went smoothly on the first day, on the second the men saw the light of what they thought was a distressed weather balloon or helicopter. As the men watched, the craft crashed and seemingly exploded in the distance. Not taking that as a sign to call this camping trip done, the men stayed for two more days. On the third there was no incident. On the fourth the men saw the same craft they thought crashed while they were out on a lake.

Jim & Jack Weiner, Charlie Foltz, Chuck Rak

Charlie, being the helpful sort, used his flashlight to signal S.O.S. A beam shot out of the craft and enveloped the four men in short order. When they awoke they were on the shore with the craft floating only feet above them. It exploded yet again before reappearing over the tree line and darting away. Despite the bizarre occurrence the trip still wasn't off.

Jim began having nightmares shortly after of his arm being examined by a creature with a long neck, large head, bulbous metallic eyes with no lids and insect-like hands. What's more, in his dreams his companions were seated on a bench on the other side of the room.

Sometime in the 1980's, at the suggestion of a Ufologist, all four men underwent regressive hypnosis. What was discovered was that all four men had a consistent description of the same being and events, with each of the men recounting humiliating physical experiments. All four were deemed mentally unstable by doctors, but they passed lie detector tests.

The Peatre Incident

In the early hours of November 29th, 1954, Gustave Gonzales and Jose Ponce were driving down the streets of Peatre, Venezuela to purchase pork from a butcher to later resell themselves that day during open markets. While they were driving, however, the street became illuminated with an intense light. The source of the light was a large metallic object blocking the road by hovering about a meter above it. Seemingly hypnotized by the light, Gonzales left the vehicle and began walking towards the UFO until he tripped over a short hairy figure.

The being had glowing eyes, retractable claws and a stiff fur coat. Gustave, apparently a very brave man, picked up the strange creature and found it to be incredibly light. It pushed him away single highhandedly, and as a fight looked to be breaking out Jose fled the scene to locate the police as more of the aliens escaped from nearby brush and leaped into their craft. One charged Gustave, who tried to attack it with a knife only to find it completely unharmed. Gustave was left with a series of scratches.

"Hairy Dwarfs" are among the oldest reported alien species but aren't nearly as common as others, so they're somewhat more obscure. There appears to be at least one other incident in Venezuela pointing to these creatures. In another attack later that year, two men tried to strike the short haired creatures with the butt of a rifle. The rifle broke.

The Hopkinsville Goblins

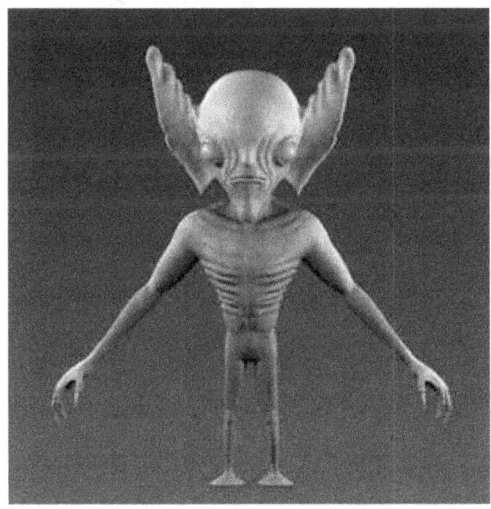

Figure 52: Hopkinsville Goblin

In August 1955, Billy Ray Taylor was visiting the Sutton family in their farmhouse near Hopkinsville, Kentucky. Because the area is so rural, the farmhouse did not utilize running water. So, a thirsty Billy ventured outside around 7:00 PM to get a drink from the water pump. That's when the trouble began.

Billy ran inside to tell the Suttons that he saw a disc-shaped aircraft covered in a series of bright lights flying in the distance. His claims were promptly dismissed as the family believed he saw a shooting star. Everyone had a good laugh until about an hour later when the family dog, tied up outside, began howling frantically and hid underneath the house. Thinking that perhaps this wasn't a shooting star, "Lucky" Sutton and Billy grabbed a pair of firearms and investigated the situation.

While searching outside, the duo saw something emerge from the trees, described as having a bulbous head, talons on its hands, large pointed ears and glowing eyes. More alarming than the bizarre appearance was its movement, as the three-foot tall creature looked to be rushing the house. The two opened fire, but the creature simply flipped over and ran in the opposite direction, seemingly bullet proof.

The two men returned to the inside of the house to discover that another member of the Sutton family had seen a similar creature peeking into the window. Throughout the night those in the house reported scratching noises from the roof, windows and doors as the creatures (which ranged in number from two to fifteen, though only two were seen together at the same time) harassed the family. The aliens were said to hover and stick to walls as well. Around 11:00 PM all eleven people in the house fled the scene and reported the incident to the Hopkinsville police.

The Hopkinsville Goblins were among the earliest widely reported UFO stories in America and abroad, so much so that the narrative has influenced several fictional stories in pop culture.

Further Evidence of Strange Alien Creatures

Figure 53: Lake Delavan Giant

Contactees and abductees may talk about giant aliens, but scientists are remaining stubbornly silent about a lost race of giants found in burial mounds near Lake Delavan, Wisconsin, in May 1912. The dig site at Lake Delavan was overseen by Beloit College and it included more than 200 effigy mounds that proved to be classic examples of 8th century Woodland Culture. But the enormous size of the skeletons and elongated skulls found in May 1912 did not fit very neatly into anyone's concept of a textbook standard. They were enormous. These were not average human beings.

Strange Skulls

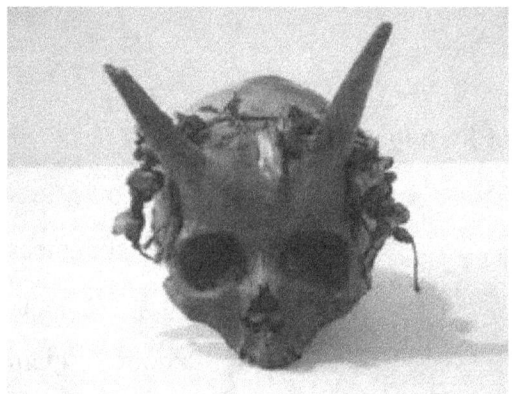

Figure 54: Certainly not the skull of a pure human

First reported in the 4 May 1912 issue of the New York Times the 18 skeletons found by the Peterson brothers on Lake Lawn Farm in southwest Wisconsin exhibited several strange and freakish features.

Their heights ranged between 7.6ft and 10 feet and their skulls "presumably those of men, are much larger than the heads of any race which inhabit America to-day." They tend to have a double row of teeth, 6 fingers, 6 toes and like humans came in different races. The teeth in the front of the jaw are regular molars. Heads usually found are elongated believed due to longer than normal life span.

"One must wonder how much can they lift if twice the size of an average human today? Are these the Giants the Bible & many other civilizations have in their history and painted on their walls? The Bible in Genesis 6:4 " There were giants in the earth in those days; and also after that, when the sons of God came in unto the daughters of men, and they bare children to them, the same became mighty men which were of old men of renown. " Now this is faulty logic to any scientist out there because of the use of religious/cultural history to fill a hole in science.

Over 200 Giant digs have been found in recent years. Giant skeleton finds have not made the local/national news since the 1950's for the most part. It seems in most people's opinion the discussion of these giant skeletons would cause people to question the theory of evolution. If anything it seems to represent a de-evolution.

In 2002, National Geographic reported a dozen Cyclops skeletons found in Greece that stood 12-15 1/2 Ft tall. That is 3 humans tall. One eye socket. Giants in history are typically cannibalistic in nature. The reason why I am bringing up giants will all tie into politics, and word happenings. Look at a basketball hoop and add 5 feet. That tall. Greek Mythology talks about war with cyclops learning they had to bring down by taking out their legs rendering them slow and helpless. American Giants (Red Hair Giants) where found with Egyptian writing on their tombs have been found in multiple locations[59].

Mystery of the Wisconsin Giants

Giant Skeletons Found.

Two skeletons, each measuring more than 7 feet in length, were discovered Friday in a gravel pit in the forest near Fond du Lac, Wis. The skulls are as large as those of two ordinary persons and the thigh bones are almost six inches longer than those of a six-foot man.

The Lake Delavan find of May 1912 was only one of dozens and dozens of similar finds that were reported in local newspapers from 1851 forward to the present day. It was not even the first set of giant skeletons found in Wisconsin.

On 10 August 1891, the New York Times reported that scientists from the Smithsonian Institution had

---

[59] © SouthMilwaukeeNow

discovered several large "pyramidal monuments" on Lake Mills, near Madison, Wisconsin. "Madison was in ancient days the center of a teeming population numbering not less than 200,000," the Times said. The excavators found an elaborate system of defensive works which they named Fort Aztalan.

"The celebrated mounds of Ohio and Indiana can bear no comparison, either in size, design or the skill displayed in their construction with these gigantic and mysterious monuments of earth -- erected we know not by whom, and for what purpose we can only conjecture," said the Times.

On 20 December 1897, the Times followed up with a report on three large burial mounds that had been discovered in Maple Creek, Wisconsin. One had recently been opened.

"In it was found the skeleton of a man of gigantic size. The bones measured from head to foot over nine feet and were in a fair state of preservation. The skull was as large as a half bushel measure. Some finely tempered rods of copper and other relics were lying near the bones."

Giant skulls and skeletons of a race of "Goliaths" have been found on a very regular basis throughout the Midwestern states for more than 100 years. Giants have been found in Minnesota, Iowa, Illinois, Ohio, Kentucky and New York, and their burial sites are similar to the well-known mounds of the Mound Builder people.

The spectrum of Mound builder history spans a period of more than 5,000 years (from 3400 BCE to the 16th CE), a period greater than the history of Ancient Egypt and all of its dynasties.

There is a "prevailing scholarly consensus" that we have an adequate historical understanding of the peoples who lived in North America during this period. However, the long record of anomalous finds like those at Lake Delavan suggests otherwise.

The Great Smithsonian Cover-Up

Has there been a giant cover-up? Why aren't there public displays of gigantic Native American skeletons at natural history museums?

The skeletons of some Mound Builders are certainly on display. There is a wonderful exhibit, for example, at the Aztalan State Park where one may see the skeleton of a "Princess of Aztalan" in the museum.

But the skeletons placed on display are normal-sized, and according to some sources, the skeletons of giants have been covered up.

Specifically, the Smithsonian Institution has been accused of making a deliberate effort to hide the "telling of the bones" and to keep the giant skeletons locked away.

In the words of Vine Deloria, a Native American author and professor of law:

"Modern day archaeology and anthropology have nearly sealed the door on our imaginations, broadly interpreting the North American past as devoid of anything unusual in the way of great cultures characterized by a people of unusual demeanor. The great interloper of ancient burial grounds, the nineteenth century Smithsonian Institution, created a one-way portal, through which uncounted bones have been spirited. This door and the contents of its vault are virtually sealed off to anyone, but government officials. Among these bones may lay answers not even sought by these officials concerning the deep past."

Two Giant Skeletons Near Potosi, WI

The January 13th, 1870 edition of the Wisconsin Decatur Republican reported that two giant, well-preserved skeletons of an unknown race were discovered near Potosi, WI by workers digging the foundation of a saw mill near the bank of the Mississippi river. One skeleton measured seven-and-a-half feet, the other eight feet. The skulls of each had prominent cheek bones and double rows of teeth. A large collection of arrowheads and "strange toys" were found buried with the remains[60].

Giant Skeleton Discovered in Maple Creek, WI

On December 20th, 1897 the New York Times reported that three large burial mounds had been discovered near Maple Creek, WI. Upon excavation, a skeleton measuring over nine feet from head to toe was discovered with finely tempered copper rods and other relics.

Giant Skeleton in West Bend, WI

A giant skeleton was unearthed outside of West Bend near Lizard Mound County Park and assembled by local farmers to a height of eight feet. More about this can be found in Washington County Paranormal: A Wisconsin Legend Trip by local author and investigator J. Nathan Couch.

While a normal-sized skeleton of a supposed mound builder (the "Princess of Aztalan") is on display at the site of several large pyramidal monuments near Madison called Aztalan State Park, the goliath remains of

---

[60] © SouthMilwaukeeNow

Wisconsin's giants have vanished along with the hundreds of others discovered throughout the Midwest.

And So

The evidence is fairly clear that humans are being visited by 7-10 foot giants with six fingers and six toes and skeletons matching these creatures are being dug up across the country. Are we dealing with the Nephilim? But what about the varying descriptions of these bedroom invaders, is it one race of aliens or more than one race. How do we answer this issue? Well perhaps we do have an answer.

A Professional View

Figure 55: Spherical UFO

On August 7, 1965 a highly respected Venezuelan gynecologist and two business associates were visiting a horse breeding farm in San Pedro de los Alton. This farm was about 30 miles south of Caracas[61].

---

[61] BUFORA Journal, Digital Archive Collection 1959-2005

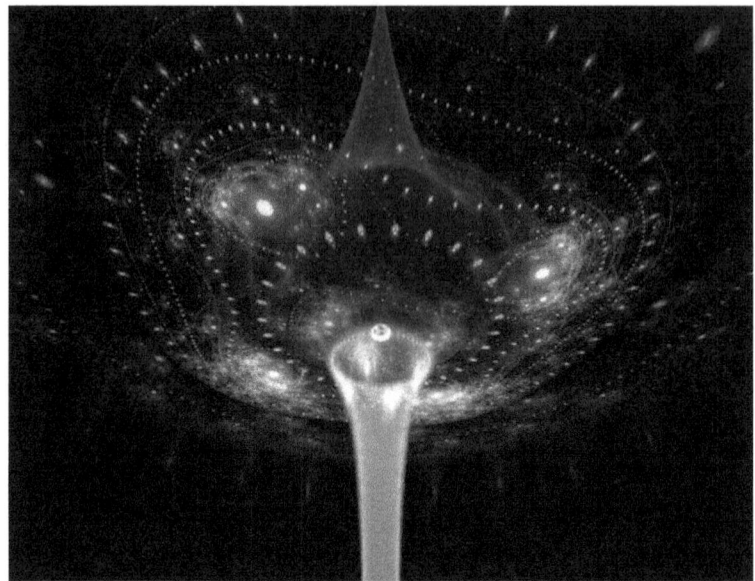

Figure 56: A reported craft sighted in Brazil

It was late afternoon when the incident took place. As the three friends discussed horse breeding, there was a bright flash in the sky. The three men looked up to see a glowing sphere drifting down from the sky. They were surrounded by a soft humming sound that seemed to be both all around them as well as inside of them. One of the men turned to run, but the gynecologist grabbed his friend and insisted that they watch what happened.

Suddenly a beam of light shot out of the side of the craft. The light was angled to the craft like a ramp and two aliens floated down the beam of light. The aliens were described as 7 feet tall, with blond hair and huge round eyes. Their clothing appeared to be made out of tinfoil. By this time the three witnesses were terrified, but they found that they were unable to escape. Once they touched the ground, the aliens came over to the three terrified witnesses and told them not to be afraid, to just calm down[62].

Figure 57: Another description of a Grey alien

Telepathically, the aliens told the three that they came from Orion to study the psyche of humans in order to adapt them to their own species. They also wanted to experiment with the possibility of interbreeding with humans in order to create a new, hybrid species.

In the somewhat lengthy discussions between the witnesses and the aliens, a number of topics were said to have been discussed. One question dealt with why some witnesses reported encountering tall, blond, blue-eyed

---

[62] Ibid

Nordic appearing aliens while other talk about small black-eyed greys.

Figure 58: Nordic Blonde Aliens

The aliens explained that there were other extraterrestrial visitors to Earth besides themselves. The short grey aliens were from a location referred to as the "outer dipper" but their purpose for coming here was unclear. The Nordics were believed to be here on a peaceful mission.

To in retrospect, these particular aliens were rather clear that they were doing experiments in interbreeding. From their level of development, they apparently do not see that we have any right to object to being the subject of these experiments and apparently neither do the other alien species that roam this planet.

CHAPTER TWELVE

A BREEDING PROGRAM

We now have, at least, circumstantial that there are alien creatures here conducting breeding experiments on humans, but how far are they willing to go to conduct their experiments? We have seen bedroom visitations and even bedroom kidnappings, but what else might they do to obtain their specimens?

Figure 59: UFO looking for a victim?

Mysterious Bleeding

On the night of April 29, 1995, a man by the name of Malcolm, his wife Samantha and their daughter Lizzie were driving across the south of France. They were traveling on the highway between Epagny and Caignes Cordon, about two hours out of Dijon where they had planned on spending some time enjoying the sights.

As they drove along the highway, they suddenly noticed a bright light that seemed to be following their car. Malcolm tried to escape from the UFO by speeding up and then slowing down, but except when there was other traffic in sight, the UFO stuck to their car like glue. Previously neither Malcolm nor Samantha believed in the reality of UFOs but after being followed for several hours they both had to admit that they were very real and that their intentions were not very friendly[63].

One of the most interesting aspects of this encounter was that the family was only two hours from Dijon when they first spotted the UFO and after driving for several more hours, they still had not reached any town. Finally, when the UFO finally disappeared, so tired that he could

---

[63] BUFORA Journal, Digital Archive Collection 1959-2005

not drive any longer, Malcolm pulled over and they slept alongside of the road.

When the family awoke, they discovered that Samantha had a severe nosebleed and Lizzie was bleeding from her anus. The family was utterly baffled as to what might have caused these issues. Then later, upon returning to England they discovered that it had taken them 3 1/ hours to cover the forty miles from Epagny to Caignes Cordon. Later investigation revealed that they could not have taken a wrong turn; the highway was straight and uncomplicated. So where had they been for over three hours?

Figure 60: Peek-a-boo I got you

Once back home, the family was plagued by disturbing dreams in which they all three saw humanoid creatures with large black eyes. Unfortunately, for them, the bad dreams were not the only manifestation to plague the family after their return from France.

Figure 61: Would you open the door?

Some nine months later, Samantha awoke in the middle of the night hearing[64] Lizzie crying but found that she was parlayed and unable to move. Unaware of his wife's problem, Malcolm stumbled from the bed and went to see what was troubling their daughter. However, before he arrived at Lizzie's bedroom, he passed a window where the curtains were open and noticed that there was someone digging up the road outside their house. Not stopping to look closer, Malcolm continued on to Lizzie's bedroom and found his daughter looking out the window and crying loudly.

As Malcolm comforted Lizzie, Samantha found that she was finally able to move, her paralysis was broken. As she stumbled out of bed, she glanced out the bedroom wind and saw people digging in the garden. Puzzled, but more

---

[64] Samantha thought it was about 4:00 AM when this incident began.

concerned about her daughter, Samantha raced down the hall and joined her husband and daughter. It was some time before any of them were able to get back to bed.

Figure 62: Not safe in your own bed

The next morning, both Samantha and Lizzie were bleeding from their rectums again. Malcolm investigated the sites where they had all seen people digging and found no trace that the soil was disturbed in any way. As for the bleeding, both Samantha and Malcolm felt that it was caused by aliens from the UFO carrying out some bizarre experiments on the two females.

Other Fluids

As we have alluded to before, these mysterious creatures do not just molest and rape females but males as well. Consider, if you will, the case of Will Parker, a 19 year old computer programmer[65]. Will and his wife Ginny were driving along a Virginia road late one night in 1974.

---

[65] BUFORA Journal, Digital Archive Collection 1959-2005

For some reason he has never been able to explain, Will pulled their car into the parking lot of a closed gas station and cut off the engine. The two just sat in the dark as if waiting for something.

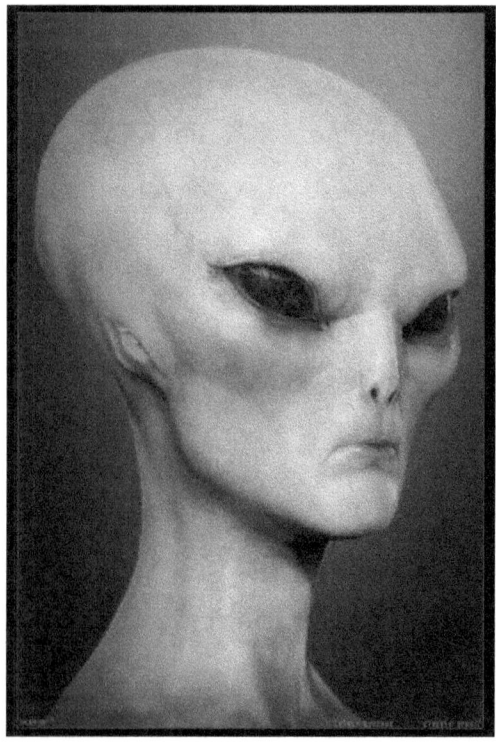

Figure 63: Grey alien

When hypnotically regressed later, Will related that the two of them just sat in the dark and chatted nervously as they waited for something – they could never explain what they were waiting for nor why they did not think it strange to sit in a dark parking lot in the middle of nowhere. After a few minutes, Ginny told him to be quiet because she thought she heard something. A few seconds later a small alien looked in the window.

Will said that Ginny was shocked and began to pray, but for some reason, Will felt very calm and he suddenly realized that he had seen these aliens before. As he watched he realized that Ginny had fallen silent, when he glanced over at her she seemed to be asleep. As if this was what they had been waiting on, the Aliens took Will from the car. As they forced him away, he kept trying to return to lock the car so that Ginny would be safe.

Figure 64: Eager for a happy ending?

The aliens forced Will around back of the closed service station where four or five more aliens were waiting. Will said that he asked the aliens where are the rest? IN response they told him not to be afraid, they were not going to hurt him and not to worry about Ginny, she would remember nothing.

Will and the aliens stood in the dark until a large UFO appeared overhead and they were lifted from the ground in the group. Gently, they led Will to a room where there was some equipment and a table. He was pushed back against the table and a device was fitted over his genitals. As soon as it was in place, he began to vibrate and in a few seconds he felt his semen being sucked out of him. He reported that he had no orgasm or sense of pleasure.

A few minutes later he found himself standing beside the car, Ginny was still asleep inside. As they had promised, she remembered nothing and his memories faded until he was hypnotically regressed.

Implantation

This next case is proof of a very unusual situation. What if human women are being used as unknowing incubators for human/alien children?

The two women involved were sisters, Janet Demerest and Karen Morgan[66]. Evidence tends to support the premise that these two human females have been

---

[66] BUFORA Journal, Digital Archive Collection 1959-2005

abducted by aliens numerous times. The first time they were abducted was 1963 when Demerest was nine years old. She and some friends had been playing near her house. The other girls formed a big circle, but, with no explanation, Demerest wandered away from the group to be by herself.

Under later hypnotic regression, she reported seeing a man with grey skin who was not very tall. He took her hand and the two of them walked through the woods until they arrived at a clearing. She said that sitting in the clearing was a UFO. She and the grey man, as she referred to him, walked up the ramp into the craft.

Inside the craft, they went into a room where there was a human woman and an odd looking girl who had greyish skin, thin arms and long slender fingers. Janet said that she had the impression that the girl had no bone structure and no ears. The man instructed Demerest to play with the girl, so Janet sat down across from her.

Janet reported that she found the girl's stare riveting and could not pull her eyes away. She was aware, however, that the man and woman were watching her reactions intently. Finally, girl hugged Janet and told her that it was time for her to go. Janet said that the grey man took her back to where he had found her.

In 1981, when Karen Morgan was 28 years old, she had an abduction experience. Under hypnotic regression, she remembered having entered a UFO and been taken to a waiting area where there were a number of benches. She was told to sit on one and wait. She noticed that there were other men and women waiting on the other benches. Some were wearing night clothes and one man was slumped over as if he was not well. A short time later, two aliens came for each human, the subjects were stripped of their clothing and they were all herded into an examination room.

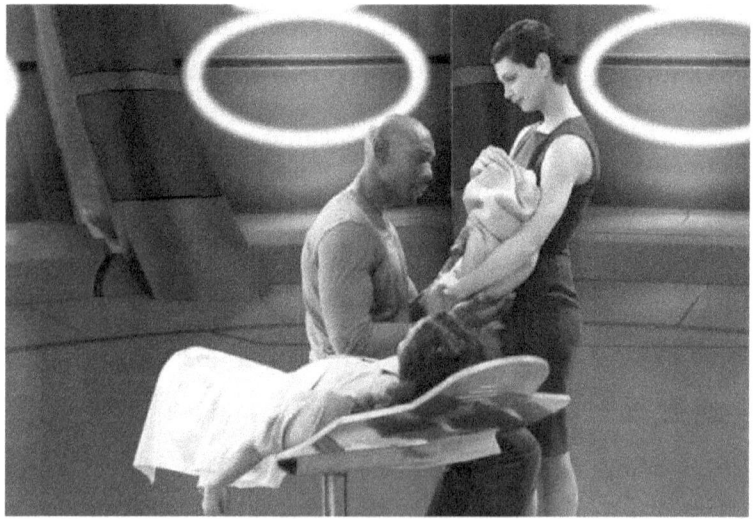

Figure 65: Implantation

Morgan said that she tried to resist what the aliens planned to do, but she was pushed along anyway. She was the last one to go into the examination room in which there were four operating tables and a shelf containing instruments. She said that she was stripped and strapped onto the table. During the examination the aliens noticed that she had braces in her mouth which they asked her to remove. She refused, but later when she awoke the braces were lying on her stomach.

Figure 66: Medical procedure

The aliens also cut out a sample of her gums for analysis, which infuriated her. She asked how much more of her they were going to take and how long it took them to study someone. They answered her that it could take years to properly study an individual. At that point a tall alien asked her to look into his eyes. She did and immediately felt as if she was being overwhelmed. Her will melted away and she realized that she could no longer fight the aliens.

Helpless, Morgan was unable to free herself as the alien proceeded to give her a thorough gynecological exam. Morgan became outraged at what was being done to her and cursed the alien in her mind. In some fashion he was very much aware of what she was doing and seemed to find it amusing. He then assured her that she would come to no harm.

Shortly after this, he proceeded to perform a smear test, but Morgan was positive that he was actually inserting an embryo into her, implanting it into her womb. She found the idea repulsive and told him so, but the alien assured her that he had to do it as it was part of a very important program. Morgan insisted that once home she would get an abortion to which the alien replied that she would not remember being implanted, that it had been done to her many times before. Slowly she felt herself giving in to the will of the alien and slowly she did forget that she had been implanted with an alien fetus.

Later, Morgan did remember that she had been implanted many times before. The very idea made her sick like she was an animal that had been bred so many times.

She somehow knew that the embryos were hybrids, part alien and part human. She remembered that sometimes the procedure was quick and sometimes it took a long period of time. On this occasion it took a long period of time. When the alien finished, he patted her gently on her belly to which she demanded that he remove his hands. Reluctantly he did so. He seemed baffled that she believed he did not have the right to do to her as he wished.

Suddenly, it was morning and Morgan was lying in her own bed. Slowly rising, she discovered that there was a gooey substance between her legs, which caused her to rush to the bathroom for a thorough shower.

Demerest recalled having undergone a similar procedure in 1987. A long needle had been inserted into her vagina and the aliens had implanted what she described as "a little round thing" into her womb. Afterward a female alien had helped her off of the table. She had been left with the over-whelming feeing that she wanted to have a baby.

During a later abduction, Morgan was shown the results of her labors when she was shown a large number of babies, she estimated between 50 and 100, lined up in boxes behind a glass panel. They were not moving and appeared to be dead, although Morgan seemed to know that they were actually alive. The babies appeared to have been suspended in some sort of liquid and were being fed through tubes by a machine.

Morgan observed that these babies, some were only fetuses, were in all stages of development. It was clear that the aliens were running a breeding program on a very large scale and that these fetuses had been taken from hundreds of women. Later she was shown through nurseries in which hundreds of babies were being tended by aliens. She was told that some of these babies were hers.

During abduction, Morgan saw an attractive man whom she knew and had the distinct impression that she was going to make love to him before gradually realizing that the man was actually an alien who was using hypnotic suggestion to sexually excite her. This brought up many questions in her mind as to how much of her daily activity was of her own volition and how much was as a result of her mind being controlled by aliens. These questions were never answered.

CHAPTER THIRTEEN

A BLOODY FASCINATION

Other Mysterious Blood Draining

One of the biggest mysteries surrounding the UFO enigma is if UFOs do represent extraterrestrial visitors, why do they operate in such secrecy? Many alleged UFO contactees and even some abductees say that the aliens are friendly and are here to help mankind. However, there is a body of evidence that extraterrestrials have a sinister, hidden agenda when dealing with Earth's inhabitants. The most obvious example of nefarious UFO activity has to be the mutilation of cattle and the raping and implanting of human females.

The evidence is mostly anecdotal that UFOs are involved with cattle mutilations, but the unusual circumstances surrounding this mystery seem to point to UFOs, or at least UFO-like activity.

Figure 67: Mutilated Cow

Over the years, strange attacks on animals and humans have been recorded and attributed to predators, other humans and even vampires. What makes these incidents similar is the general lack of blood found on the bodies or in the surrounding area. Primitive man believed that blood was sacred, the source of life in all creatures. When you lost your blood, you lost your life. So to them, it made sense that the life force must be contained in blood.

The Old Testament is a good example of ancient beliefs regarding blood. Leviticus 17:14 states, that *"the life of every living creature is its blood."* The verse goes on to say that it is forbidden for anyone to eat blood because it is the source of all life.

Because of these early beliefs, man has always had a superstitious horror when dealing with unusual attacks that involve an unusual loss of blood. Throughout history, there have been numerous reports of strange attacks and mutilations that seem to go beyond normal animal predators.

In 1874 near Cavan, Ireland, for several months something killed as many as thirty sheep a night, biting their throats and draining the blood. Amazingly, there were rarely any tracks found around the dead animals.

Figure 68: Mutilated Cow in New Mexico

In 1905 at Great Badminton, Avon, sheep were again the target for attacks. A police sergeant in Gloucestershire was quoted in the London Daily Mail, "*I have seen two of the carcasses myself and can say definitely that it is impossible for it to be the work of a dog.*

Dogs are not vampires, and do not suck the blood of a sheep, and leave the flesh almost untouched."

In a single night in March of 1906, near the town of Guildford, Great Britain, fifty-one sheep were killed when their blood was drained from bite wounds to the throats. Local residents formed search parties to hunt down whatever was killing their livestock, but nothing was ever caught, and the killings remain a mystery.

Events of this kind have probably occurred regularly throughout history. The cases that have received media attention are those involving a large number of deaths, but there are probably hundreds of smaller attacks that have gone unnoticed over the years.

These strange livestock attacks are eerily similar to the recent attacks by the so-called Chupacabra, which means "goat sucker" in Spanish Confining itself chiefly to the southern hemisphere, the Chupacabra has been blamed for numerous attacks on small animals. The animals have had their throats bitten and their blood sucked out by the creature that reportedly stands on two legs, has large black or red eyes and is about four feet tall. Unlike past killings, the Chupacabra has been seen by shocked eyewitnesses whose descriptions seem to describe an animal that superficially resembles the "Grays" of flying saucer lore.

As in past cases, attempts to track down the Chupacabra have met with failure. If history is any indication, the Chupacabra will never be caught, and the strange events will remain a mystery. It is as if the mystery mutilators appear out of thin air, do their damage, and then, just as quickly, disappear again.

The mutilation of cattle seems to involve a different set of circumstances then past vampire-like attacks on livestock. While cattle mutilations almost always involve the complete draining of blood, physical mutilation of the flesh is so apparent that seasoned ranchers are shocked by the unusual nature of the deaths.

No one really knows when the first unusual cattle mutilations began. Records show that in the middle of 1963, a series of livestock attacks occurred in Haskell County, Texas. In a typical case, an Angus bull was found with its throat slashed and a saucer-sized wound in its stomach. The attacks were attributed to a wild beast of some sort, a "vanishing varmint." As the attacks continued through the Haskell County area, the unknown attacker assumed mythic proportions and a new name was created, "The Haskell Rascal." Whatever was responsible for the mutilations was never caught, and the attacks slowly stopped.

Throughout the following decade though, there would be similar reports of attacks on livestock. The most prominent of these infrequent reports was the mutilation death of a horse named Lady, in 1967. Area residents of southern Colorado reported UFO activity the night before Lady was found dead, and the consensus was that the unknown craft were somehow responsible.

In 1973 the modern cattle mutilation wave can be said to have begun in earnest. It is interesting to note that a huge UFO flap was occurring across the country in 1973, with many sightings taking place in the same areas that cattle mutilations were happening. In November of 1974, rumors began to connect the sighting of UFOs with mutilated cows that were being found in large numbers in various Minnesota counties. Dozens of UFOs were reported in Minnesota and dozens of cattle were found dead and mutilated. Although the sightings and mutilations were never correlated, many felt that the number of sightings was added proof that the UFOs were somehow involved.

In 1975, an unprecedented onslaught of strange deaths spread across the western two-thirds of the United States. Mutilation reports peaked in that year, accompanied by accounts of UFOs and unidentified helicopters.

By 1979, numerous livestock mutilations were also being reported in Canada, primarily in Alberta and Saskatchewan. In 1980, there was an increase in activity in the United States. Mutilations have been reported less frequently since that year, though this may be due in part to an increased reluctance to report mutilations on the part of ranchers and farmers. In the 1990's the mutilations have continued. In the United States, over ten thousand animals have reportedly died under unusual circumstances.

Because of the strange nature of the killings, wild stories and rumors have surfaced over the years in an attempt to explain what is really going on. Chief among these are stories that aliens are harvesting cattle at night for their evil purposes. The extraterrestrials' preoccupation with cattle is apparently due to the fact that the ET's absorb nutrients through the skin. The blood that they acquire from the cattle is mixed with hydrogen peroxide, which kills the foreign bacteria in the mixture, and is "painted" on their skin, allowing absorption of the required nutrients. Supposedly human blood is preferred by the aliens, but cattle blood can be altered to serve the same purpose.

While it may seem far-fetched that animal blood could be used in place of human blood, recent scientific discoveries seem to confirm that animal blood can be altered for human transfusions. According to The Observer, a weekly paper in Great Britain, the scientists who helped engineer the first cloned sheep are reportedly close to generating human blood plasma from animals.

PPL Therapeutics, the Scottish firm that helped Edinburgh's Roslyn Institute clone a sheep, is developing the means to replace the plasma genes of sheep and cows with the human equivalent. PPL told the paper it plans to raise herds of the animals and manufacture plasma from the proteins extracted from the animals. The Observer quoted Dr. Ron James, the firm's managing director, as saying. "Only 5 percent of Britain's population regularly gives blood. Genetically modified animals could produce 10,000 times more plasma a year than a human donor."

In 1991 DNX Corp., a Princeton-based biotechnology firm, announced that it had developed genetically engineered, transgenic pigs that produce large quantities of recombinant human hemoglobin. When commercialized, DNX's blood substitute could provide a cost-effective, virtually unlimited alternative to the human blood supply that is entirely free from the threat of contamination by infectious agents that cause diseases such as AIDS and hepatitis.

In addition, DNX's recombinant hemoglobin-based transfusion product will be universally compatible with all blood types, eliminating the need for blood typing and cross matching, and will have improved shelf-life and storage characteristics. DNX's announcement was made to the 1991 World Congress on Cell and Tissue Culture in Anaheim, Calif., by John Logan, vice president of research at DNX. Perhaps the wild stories are not so far-fetched after all.

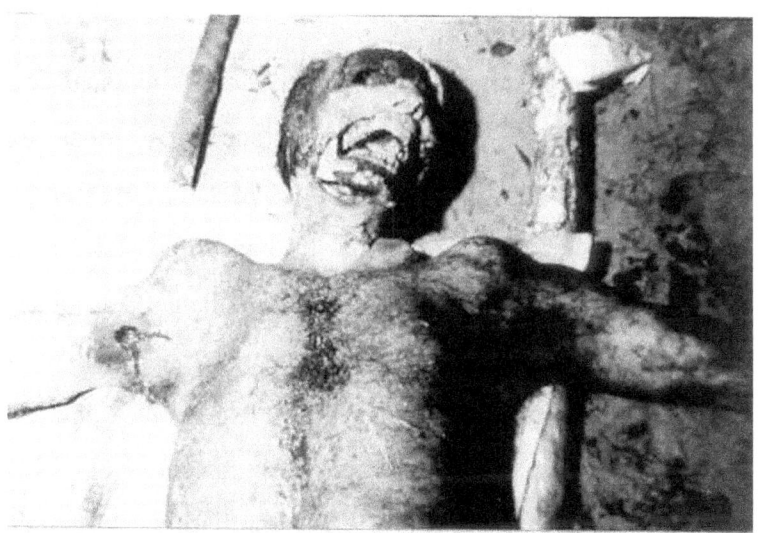

Figure 69: Body of a man found mutilated

If the stories are true, some would ask why aren't the aliens catching and mutilating humans instead of animals. The truth could be that human mutilations and deaths are occurring on a regular basis, but that the stories are too horrible to contemplate. The mutilated body of a man was found near the Guarapiranga Reservoir in Brazil on 29th. The wounds were similar to those found on the mutilated animals.

If murderous, UFO-related human mutilations have taken place, they have either gone unrecognized for what they really are, or have been adeptly covered up by official intervention. Thousands of people worldwide disappear every year, never to be seen again. A majority of these disappearances can be attributed to homicides or other more common situations.

However, some disappearances are so unusual and unexplained that more disturbing scenarios must be examined. In 1956 at the White Sands Missile Test Range, an Air Force major reported that he had witnessed a disk shaped flying object kidnap Sgt. Jonathan P. Louette. Louette was missing for three days when his mutilated body was found in the dessert near the test range. Louette's genitals had been removed and his rectum cored out with surgical precision. Like many cattle mutilations, Louette's eyes had been removed and all of his blood was missing. The Air Force filed a report stating that Sgt. Louette had died of exposure after being lost in the dessert.

The late Leonard H. Stringfield, a former Air Force intelligence officer wrote in his self-published book, UFO

Crash/Retrievals, Status Report No. 6, about the testimony given by a "high ranking Army officer" whom Stringfield says he has known for several years and who is allegedly a "straight shooter." The officer claimed that while he was in Cambodia during the Vietnam War, his Special Operations group was involved in a fire fight with aliens, whom the soldiers came across sorting human body parts and sealing them into large bins. Subsequently the unit was held for several days and interrogated under hypnosis. The officer claimed that he and his men were given cover memories which only began to surface years later.

The implications here are staggering. If this story is true, then the possibility exists that military and government officials are aware of the aliens' interests in the physiological makeup of the human body.

In 1989, the mysterious death of a man a decade earlier came to the attention of the MUFON State Director of Idaho, Don Mason. According to the report, in 1979, two hunters in the Bliss and Jerome area of Idaho stumbled across the almost nude body of a man that had been hideously mutilated. The body's sexual organs had been removed, its lips were sliced off, and the blood had been drained. Although the body was found in very rugged country, its bare feet were not marked, and no other tracks, animal or human were evident. After the police were notified, an intensive search was mounted and the man's possessions were recovered miles from where the body was found. No one knows how the body ended up where it was found, or even more importantly, what happened to him. It should be noted that this area over the years, has had many unexplained UFO reports and cattle mutilations.

In Westchester county New York, in 1988, several morgues were broken into late at night. Fresh human bodies had undergone mutilations involving partial removal of the face and total removal of the eyes, stomach, thyroid gland and genitals. An assistant medical examiner, who had broken the silence concerning the case, stated that checks were immediately run on the employees who were on duty at the morgues. No links connecting morgue employees with the crimes were found. While there is no evidence that UFOs were responsible for the bizarre incidents, once again we see human bodies being mutilated in the same ways that cattle and other animals are being mutilated.

Another interesting case that has received little publicity in the United States is the Brazilian Guarapiranga reservoir case. Brazilian ufologist Encarnacion Zapata Garcia and Dr. Rubens Goes uncovered a series of sensational photographs obtained from police files. The photos are of a dead man whose injuries are similar to the wounds of countless UFO-related animal mutilation cases. The body had been found near Guarapiranga reservoir on September 29, 1988. The name of the man has been withheld from the media and UFO investigators at the request of his relatives. After studying the photos, Encarnacion Garcia was impressed with how similar the wounds of the body were to those found on the carcasses of so many mutilated animals. The initial police report noted that the body, although extremely mutilated, showed no signs of struggle or the application of bondage of any kind.

The body appeared to be in good condition. Rigor mortis had not set in and it was estimated that the victim had been killed approximately 48 to 72 hours previously. There were no signs of animal predation or decay which might be expected. Strangely, there was no odor to the body. Bleeding from the wounds had been minimal. In fact, it was noted that there was a general lack of blood found in the body or on the ground around the body. Police photos show that the flesh and lips had been removed from around the mouth, as is common in cattle and other animal mutilations. An autopsy report stated that "the eyes and ears were also removed and the mouth cavity was emptied." Removal of these body parts, including the tongue as here, is common enough in animal mutilation cases

The "surgery" appeared to have been done by someone familiar with surgical procedures. The lack of profuse bleeding suggested the use of a laser-like instrument producing heat, thus immediately cauterizing the edge of the wounds. The autopsy report states that, "The axillary regions on both sides showed soft spots where organs had been removed. Incisions were made on the face, internal thorax, abdomen, legs, arms, and chest. Shoulders and arms have perforations of 1 to 1.5 inches in diameter where tissue and muscles were extracted. The edges of the perforations were uniform and so was their size. The chest had shrunk due to the removal of internal organs."

The autopsy report continues, "*You also find the removal of the belly button leaving a 1.5 inch hole in the abdomen and a depressed abdominal cavity showing the removal of the intestines.*" The report also noted the victims' scrotum had been removed, and that the anal orifice had been extracted with a large incision about 3 to 6 inches in diameter.

It is significant that the police and medical examiners were convinced the holes found in the head, arms, stomach, anus and legs were not produced by bullet wounds. What is most disturbing about the anal incision and the extraction of anal and digestive tract tissue is that it is a carbon copy of the surgery seen in so many UFO-related animal mutilation cases.

While no evidence linking the Guarapiranga reservoir mutilation case with UFOs has been found, Brazilian ufologist and police have hinted that there may be at least a dozen or more cases similar to this one. In fact, Brazil has had past incidents where UFOs have reportedly attacked people, and possibly taking blood from them.

The July 12, 1977 edition of the JORNAL DA BAHIA reported that, "A fantastic story of a flying object emitting a strong light and sucking blood from people, circulated from mouth to mouth among the population of the counties of Braganca, Vizeu and Augusto Correa in Para', where many people fear leaving their homes during the night so they won't get caught by the vampire-like light from the strange object which, according to information, already has caused the death of two men. No one knows how the story started, but the truth is that it reached Bele'm and grabbed headlines in the local newspapers."

Months later, on October 8, the newspaper O LIBERAL launched the first in a series of reports, about the

Chupa-Chupa (suck-suck) phenomenon. "Sucking animal attacks men and women in the village of Vigia: A strange phenomenon has been occurring for several weeks in the village of Vigia, more exactly in the Vila Santo Antonio de Imbituba about 7 kilometers from highway PA-140, with the appearance of an object which focus a white light over people, immobilizing them for around an hour, and sucks the breasts of the women leaving them bleeding.

The object, known by the locals as "Bicho Voador" (Flying Animal), or "Bicho Sugador" (Sucking Animal), has the shape of a rounded ship and attacks people in isolation. One of the victims, among many in the area, was Mrs. Rosita Ferreira, married, 46 years old, resident of Ramal do Triunfo, who a few days ago was sucked by the light on the left breast, and passed out. Increasingly it looked like she was dealing with a nightmare, feeling as if there were some claws trying to hold her. She was attacked around 3:30 in the morning. Another victim was the lady known as "Chiquita," who was also sucked by the strange object with her breast becoming bloody, but without leaving any mark

Compared to reports of mysterious animal attacks and mutilations, reports involving humans are somewhat rare. The probable reason is that many such incidents involving people are not recognized for what they are or the victims are forced to remain silent. Based on the evidence presented herein, the possibility is that a massive cover-up by officials world-wide exists to hide the fact that something is preying on humans.

If we consider that extraterrestrials are visiting Earth, the likely reason for such visitations is scientific exploration.

CHAPTER FOURTEEN
BILL ENGLISH AND GRUDGE 13

This author has been doing a radio talk show[67] for over twenty years and has interviewed hundreds of individuals with an involvement in the UFO field. One of those guests interviewed on the show was a former Army Captain by the name of Bill English, son of an Arizona state legislator and former captain in the Green Berets

Captain English became involved in the UFO mystery as a result of his service as the commander of a Special Forced A Team in Vietnam. It has now come to light that during the Vietnam War there was a great deal of UFO contact between our military aircraft and what are referred to as UFOs. Most of these encounters were immediately classified.

---

[67] The Ken Hudnall Show is currently internet based and heard at http://www.kenhudnall.com. The interview can be heard in the membership section of the website.

According to Bill English on one occasion, a B-52 Bomber reported that it was under attack by a UFO over the jungles of Vietnam. Communications had been received from the B-52 before it went down to the effect that it was, "...under attack by a UFO.." a "...large light...". Then all communication ceased.

Figure 70: B-52

Captain English was ordered to take his Special Forces A Team and recover classified information and equipment from the downed bomber and if possible, determine the cause of the crash. He was also ordered to take pictures of everything.

After an arduous trek through the jungle, Captain English found the crash site. The huge Bomber was found intact, sitting in the Jungle. There was no swath indicative of a crash landing. Only the bottom of the fuselage showed any damage, there was no damage to the underside of the engine pods. Most interestingly, the door was still locked from the inside. The team had to blow the door to enter. Inside the craft, the crew members were dead and mutilated in much the same manner as the mutilated cattle found across the southwest United States.

After blasting their way in, the team found the crew dead. They were still in their seats and harnesses, but 'horribly mutilated.' Despite the damage to their bodies, there was very little blood present on the floor of the aircraft. After photographing the scene and collecting items on their retrieval list, the Special Forces team set off charges causing bombs still on board the aircraft to explode and incinerate the bodies inside.

According to the interview conducted by Bill English[68] Bill was honorably discharged in 1973 while overseas. He remained in Germany with his wife until she was transferred to RAF Chicksands' Department of Defense

---

[68] The Ken Hudnall Show was originally called Adventure Radio when it started in Anaheim California.

Schools. Bill's wife was a GS-9 (Teacher). After the couple arrived at Chicksands, English ran into a former Commanding Officer working for the NSA. He offered Bill a job at a listening post known as the 'elephant cage.' English accepted the position and remained there until July of 1976.

According to Bill, "It was my job to analyze the translated transcripts of radio transmissions that had been received from Soviet bloc nations through the listening post at Chicksands. We monitored military frequencies mostly. I had to assign what we called a probability rating to the material and create a possible scenario that might result from the transmission or might have resulted in the transmission. Say, for example, if we received information that so-and-so was on vacation somewhere, and then we heard a phone call made from a certain location, we'd compare the two and get an indication whether or not this gentleman really was on vacation or not."

Grudge 13 Report

Near the end of June, 1976, English received a 625 page report to examine and evaluate. He identifies the report as Grudge/Blue Book Report 13. After examining the report and all of the attachments, Bill leaves us with the impression that he assigned a high probability rating to the report which indicated that UFOs were of extraterrestrial origin. He says that decision was greatly influenced by the inclusion of photos associated with a classified military mission that occurred around May of 1970. That mission discussed I this report was the one commanded by English when he was sent to recover classified material from the downed B-52 in Vietnam.

Apart from the inclusion of photos taken by the Special Forces Team in Laos, the report contained some very upsetting and disturbing information. The human mutilation case of Sergeant Lovette is a good example. In March of 1956, Air Force Sergeant Jonathan P. Lovette was with Major William Cunningham of the United States Air Force Missile Command. The two were at White Sands Missile Range looking for debris from a missile test. Sergeant Lovette was separated from Major Cunningham for a brief period of time when Cunningham heard him scream.

Cunningham ran over a dune and saw Lovette being dragged aboard a disc-shaped object by a snake-like device wrapped around his legs. Cunningham ran back to his vehicle and radioed news of the incident to Mission Control. Search parties were dispatched to find Lovette.

After Cunningham was debriefed, he was admitted to the White Sands Base Dispensary for observation. Three days into the search, Lovette's nude body was located ten miles downrange.

According to English, "The body had been mutilated; the tongue had been removed from the lower portion of the jaw. An incision had been made just under the tip of the chin and extended all the way back to the esophagus and larynx. He had been emasculated and his eyes had been removed... (Censored for disturbing content)... There was no sign of blood within the system. The initial autopsy report confirmed that the system had been completely drained of blood and that there was no vascular collapse due to death by bleeding... When the body was found there were a number of dead predatory type birds within the area who apparently had died after trying to eat the sergeant's body."

The Aftermath

Less than a month after he first received the Grudge/Blue Book Report 13, English reported to work only to find himself being escorted to the Base Commander's Office by security personnel. Colonel Robert Black informed him that his services were no longer needed and that he was being immediately expelled from the UK. English was placed on an aircraft at RAF Lakenheath and flown back to the USA without the opportunity to contact his wife or anyone else. Once home, he was given a plane ticket back to Arizona. Bill's wife was left with the impression that he had simply abandoned her and he said that he never was allowed to see his wife or children again.

Two years later, Colonel Black and his Operations Sergeant appeared at Bill's place of business in Tucson, AZ. Black told English that they had also been given the boot by the military because of Grudge/Blue Book Report 13 and that he had a plan to get even with them. Black claimed to have information about an enormous alien craft that was buried at the White Sands Missile Range in New Mexico. He wanted English to help him and his former Operations Sergeant find it and expose the Government Cover-Up. Bill agreed to help, sold his business and threw his money in with theirs.

According to English "We purchased a van, which we outfitted with desert tires, marine radar, listening devices, magnetometers and some pretty flaky video cameras of the time. We rendezvoused and traveled along the perimeter of WSMR, and in certain areas we would cross into the test range and look around. Ultimately we wound up in White Sands National Park. From there we drove onto the range. Toward sunset, I was walking on the range about 1,000 yards in front of the vehicle. Black and his sergeant were both in it at the time. I heard a rather familiar sound, and screamed 'Incoming!' and went face first into the dirt. The next thing I know, the van is blowing up. I think they fired a rocket. Then there are helicopters all over the place, and I am running for my life, literally. I made it back to Tucson on foot."

After a series of quickly calculated steps and help from friends, English went into hiding. English began telling his story to most any serious UFO Researcher that would listen. This got his name out before the public and made the possibility of any additional assassination attempts unlikely.

When living in New York City in the 1990s, this author was told a very interesting story by another author. He said he was investigating someone he had been turned on to by a law enforcement friend. It had been discovered that bodies in local morgues and funeral homes were found to be strangely mutilated. These particular bodies were coming from parts of New York City and Westchester

County[69]. What was interesting was that the medical reports on these bodies, which were mostly unidentified, made no mention of the mutilations.

Could it be that the kidnapping and mutilation of humans is much more wide spread than admitted and that the evidence is being covered up through a network of "friendly' doctors and morticians? It would certainly explain a lot.

At Fort Benning, during my military service days I was made aware of an unusually large number of missing children and the discovery of numerous dead children found inside the tunnels beneath certain training areas on some of the older military posts across the country. It should also be noted that Bill English stated that Grudge 13 also addressed missing children.

One of the cases he discussed that he stated was part of the Grudge 13 Report was known as the Darlington Farm Case. As reported by English, "October 1953. A man, his wife and their 13 year old son were sitting down at dinner table. As they sat there the lights in the farm house began to dim. Dogs and animals raised ruckus on outside.

---

[69] I was made aware of other areas where similarly mutilated bodies were turning up, but I was unable to follow up on these stories.

13 year old boy got up from dinner table to see what was going on.

A few minutes later the ball called his mother and father to come look at the funny light in the sky. Father and mother went out onto the porch. When they got out on the porch one of the dogs broke loose from leash beside house and came running around front. Boy began chasing it into the open field."

"As mother and father watched the light come down from the sky, they described it as a round ball of fire and it began to hover over the field where the boy and dog had run to. As they stood and watched, the mother and father heard the boy start screaming for help whereupon the father grabbed his shotgun which was right next to the door and began to run out into the field with the mother following. When the father got to the field he saw his son being carried away by what looked like little men, into this huge fiery looking object. As it took off the father fired several rounds at the object, to no avail. They found the dog; its head had been crushed but no sign of the boy or any other footprints of the little men who apparently carried him off."

"Father called the Darlington police and they immediately came out to investigate. The official report read that the boy had run off and was lost in the forest which bordered the farm. Within 48 hours the Air Force made the determination that the family was to be relocated. The mother and father were picked up by Air Force (personnel) and all personal belongings and possessions were loaded into U.S. Air Force trucks and moved to a northwestern relocation site. The mother was in shock and had to go through a great deal of psychotherapy and deprogramming as did father. One interesting aspect about this case was classification under Air Force report which read it was a genuine CE 3 and that for the good of national security the mother and father had been relocated to relocation zones Z21-14. Not sure whether this indicated map grid coordinates or latitude longitude."

Project Grudge/ Project Blue Book

A series of PROJECT GRUDGE/BLUE BOOK reports have been released over the years in connection with the USAF's investigation into UFO's which was supposedly terminated with the release of the Condon report in the late 1960's. Reports 1 through twelve of GRUDGE/BLUE BOOK were generally innocuous and contained no classified or truly sensitive material.

There was a final report, #14 which was widely circulated and about which an entire book was written entitled: *Flying Saucers: An Analysis of the Air Force Project Blue Book Special Report No. 14* by Leon Davidson[70].

It should also be noted that English, through contacts he still maintains has determined that the US government 'most definitely' supports a 'project dealing specifically with UFO's and captured aliens'. According to what he has learned, the US government captured a trio of aliens, and that as of mid-1981, one of the beings was still alive in captivity. English also claims that, "at one point in the early 1950's until the mid-1960's the Air Force maintained relocation and debriefing colonies for people who had experienced close encounters of the 3rd and 4th kind. They were Isolated for all intents and purposes for the rest of their lives." He doubts that these colonies are still in existence.

English dictated 2 audio cassettes outlining whit he remembered from the Grudge 13 report. These audio cassettes were transcribed into hand written notes by another person. The Information contained therein Indicated what had been suspected all along: that the U.S.

---

[70]Davidson, Leon, Flying Saucers: An Analysis of the Air Force Project Blue Book Special Report, No. 14, Blue-Book Publishers; 64 Prospect St., White Plains, New York 10606

Government was Involved In the greatest deception In the history of mankind and that not only did flying saucers exist, but that the government had several in secret storage and had captured at least 3 live aliens. This author was allowed to hear parts of the cassettes which led to his having English appear on his show.

The following is a summary of what Bill English remembers from what he read during that day in June, 1977 of PROJECT GRUDGE/BLUE BOOK REPORT NO. 13.

- He was handed a box containing a diplomatic pouch under lock and key system. Lock had been opened, pouch was easily accessed. It was a standard diplomatic couriers pouch marked American Embassy Couriers, contained pouch serial number JL327Delta. Inside a publication with red tape which indicated code red security precautions and an Air Force disposition form. Disposition form was a standard white page copy; the title was 'Analysis Report'.
- Further down the form was the annotation 'Analyze enclosed report under code red measures, give abstract breakdown and report on validity. Observe all code red measures. Analysis required immediately'.

- Underneath that annotation were a series of dashes then the letters NDF then another series of dashes. Below that, lower left hand corner were the initials WGB.
- The document in the pouch measured approximately 8" by 11" with gray cover. Heavily bound, paper back style similar to technical manuals. Across the center front it read, "Grudge/Blue Book Report No. 13". It was dated 1953-(1963).
- In the lower right hand corner was AFSN 2246-3. In upper left hand corner was the word 'annotated'. Across the front upper right hand corner to lower left hand corner was red tape indicating code red security measures.
- Across the front was stamped in red ink 'Top Secret Need To Know Only Crypto Clearance 14 Required'. Inside front cover upper left hand corner were hand written notations in ink which were blacked out by black felt pen.
- Inside cover sheet was basically the same information as the cover. Second page was title page. Next page after that was an appendix with numerous notations made In It. Notations dealt with

Inserts of what appeared to be photos-and additional notes. At bottom of the third page it read G/BV Page 1 of 624 pages. Title page was subject letter. There was a long list of appendices which Bill did not completely remember. Title. Some notes on the practical applications of the Worst Nemo equations.

- **Table of Contents,**
    - Part 1, "On the design of generators to accomplish strain free molecular translation"
    - Part 2, "the generation of space time discontinuums, closed, open and folded"
    - Part 3, "on the generation of temporary pseudo acceleration locas"

        - Part 1, Chapter 1 "design criteria for a simple generator and control system referring to equation 17 appendix A"

    - Part 2, Chapter 1 "Continuation of Einstein's Theory of Relativity to final conclusion"

- Part 3, Chapter 1 "Possible applications of Einstein theory of relativity at conclusion".

- Part 1, Chapter 2, "Reports of UFO encounters, classification 'Close Encounters of the 1st Kind' subtitle sightings and witnesses"
- Part 2, Chapter 2, 'Close Encounters of- the 2nd Kind' subtitle UFO sightings witnessed within close proximity.
- Part 3, Chapter 2, "Close Encounters of the 3rd Kind", subtitle UFO encounters and extraterrestrial life forms witnessed and personal encounters. Subtitle/colonies relocation thereof"

- Case histories.

  - Chapter 3 Part 1, "Military Encounters with UFO's"

- Chapter 3 Part 2, "Military Reports Concerning Sightings on Radar and Electronic Surveillance of UFO's.

- Subsection 2, Analysis Report, J. Allen Hynek, Lt. Col. Friend.

- Appendix continued on for about 5 pages.

- Opening subject page consisted of a report of the findings as written by Lt. Col. Friend and his analysis.

The particular version of the Grudge 143 Report was annotated with inserts that were added to this copy after it had been initially printed. The sections that he remembered the best were the photographs and the reports concerning captive sights of various UFO's to include Mexico, Sweden, United States, and Canada.

There were also what was then classified Close Encounters of the 3rd Kind. It was made very clear that these people whom it was determined had genuine CE 3's were moved in the middle of the night by Air Force personnel and relocated to various sites in the Midwest and northwest parts of the United States. In many cases these people experienced physical ailments from exposure to various types of radiation.

Care of Victims

According to the report there were at least 4 relocation sites across the United States. Depending upon which type of encounter these people had, the report indicated that there were extensive medical facilities available at these relocation sites to deal with all medical emergencies up to an including radiation poisoning. The report mentioned a site located in the Utah-Nevada area, but no indication of its purpose or what it was for.

The Report gave clear Indication of reports of human mutilations, most notably was a case witnessed by Air Force personnel in which an Air Force Sgt. EE-6 by the name of Jonathon P. Lovette was observed being taken captive aboard what appeared to be a UFO at the White Sands Missile Test Range In New Mexico. This abduction took place in March of 1956 at about 0300 local and was witnessed by Major William Cunningham of the United States Air Force Missile Test Command near Holloman Air Force Base.

Major Cunningham and Sgt. Lovette were out in a field downrange from the launch sites looking for debris from a missile test when Sgt. Lovette went over the ridge of a small sand dune and was out of sight for a time. Major Cunningham heard Sgt. Lovette scream in what was described as terror or agony. The major, thinking the Sgt. had been bitten by a snake or something ran over the crest of the dune and saw Sgt. Lovette being dragged into what appeared to him and was described as being a silvery disk like object which hovered in the air approximately 15 to 20 feet.

Major Cunningham described what appeared to be a long snake-like object which was wrapped around the sergeants legs and was dragging him to the craft. Major Cunningham admittedly froze as the sergeant was dragged inside the disc and observed the disc going up into the sky very quickly. Major Cunningham got on the Jeep radio and reported the incident to Missile Control whereupon Missile Control confirmed a radar sighting. Search parties went out into the field looking for Sgt. Lovette. Major Cunningham's report was taken and he was admitted to the White Sands Base Dispensary for observation.

The search for Sgt. Lovette was continued for 3 days at the end of which his nude body was found approximately 10 miles downrange. The body had been mutilated; the tongue had been removed from lower portion of the Jaw. An incision had been made just under the tip of the chin and extended all the way back to the esophagus and larynx. He had been emasculated and his eyes had been removed. Also, his anus had been removed and there were comments in the report on the apparent surgical skill of the removal of these items including the genitalia.

The report commented that the anus and genitalia had been removed 'as though a plug' which In the case of the anus extended all the way up to the colon. There was no sign of blood within the system. The initial autopsy report confirmed that the system had been completely drained of blood and that there was no vascular collapse due to death by bleeding.

Sub comment was added that this was unusual because anybody who dies or has complete loss of blood there is vascular collapse. Also noted was that when the body was found there were a number of dead predatory type birds within the area who apparently had died after trying to partake of the sergeant body. There were a number of extremely grisly black and white photos. From all indications the body had been exposed to the elements for at least a day or two. The New Mexico sun in the desert is extremely hot and debilitating under normal circumstances.

In this section of the report it also indicated that there were numerous occasions in which a UFO tracked alongside of a fired missile and on one occasion said missile was observed being taken aboard a UFO while in flight. The speeds indicated were absolutely phenomenal.

(English's father had told him privately that on more than one occasion he had personally tracked what they termed as 'foo fighters'. English' father was an electronic engineer by profession and was fairly well versed on electronics engineering and design and on more than one occasion he was involved in telemetry programming of missies. English's father is currently a state legislator in Arizona.)

The report also indicated that there were a number of recovery teams that were activated specifically for the purpose of recovering any and all evidence of UFO's and UFO sightings. Most notably recorded in publication was what they called Recovery Team Alpha. It was reported that Alpha had been extremely active in a number of area and on certain occasions had traveled outside of the continental United States. Alpha was based out of Wright-Patterson Air Force Base and was on the move constantly.

Further information in the report consisted of such things as reported sightings and where air force planes had been destroyed or had combat encounters or had been attacked by UFO's. Also there were autopsy reports of various human mutilations.

About midway through the report came a section which dealt specifically with photographs. Each photo was labeled and attached to certain reports. A number of photos in there dealt with a recovery program of some type that took place in the southwestern part of the United States. They did not give a location name but they did give grid coordinates for that area. There is no clear indication to exactly where it was. The photos dealt with special teams that were called in to recover a crashed UFO. It also dealt with alien bodies and autopsy reports, autopsy type photographs, high quality, color, 8x10, 5x7.

Photo number 1 showed an alien being on an autopsy table which is a metal table with runnels and traps underneath to trap fluid and feces. Body appeared to be a little short of 4 feet. Table was about 7 foot. No clothing on body, no genitalia, body completely heterous, head was rounded cranium, slightly enlarged, eyes almond shaped, slits where nose would be, extremely small mouth, receding chin line, holes where ears would be.

Photo was taken at angle, side view, looking at body from 45° elevation, left hand was .visible, head was facing to left, body was right to left position (head on right, feet on left), eyes were closed appeared oriental-looking and almond shaped, left hand slight longer than normal, wrist coming down Just about 2 to 3 Inches above the knees. Wrists appeared to be articulated in a fashion that allowed a double Joint with 3 digit fingers. Wrist was very slender. There was no thumb. A palm was almost non-existent. The three fingers were direct extension from the wrist.

Color of the skin was bluish gray, dark bluish gray. At base of the body there was a darker color; Indicating body was dead for some time. Body fluid or blood had settled to base of body. This indicated that body had been examined before beginning autopsy.

Picture showed beginning stages of autopsy, following standard procedure, body was slit from crotch to Just under chin and green viscous liquid was in evidence. There were internal organs but these could not be identified. Photos thereafter concerned specific areas of internal organs of what appeared as small cluster of a multi-valve heart or at least 2 hearts within the cadaver.

No accurate description of autopsy report or what was found within corpse accompanying photos. Indication that there was no stomach or digestive track per se. Later analysis showed that fluid within body was chlorophyll-based liquid which apparently dealt with photosynthesis or similar process. The report theorized that nourishment was taken in through mouth, however since there is no digestive track or anything of this nature, the waste products were excreted through skin.

One section of report did specify that cadavers were extremely odorous, but this could be accounted for by either deterioration or a number of things, but theory was that waste was excreted through pores of skin. They could only theorize in this report because there was no xenobiology.

A report by Dr. J. Allen Hynek indicated that he had also studied the information provided by this particular case and that he felt that it was indeed a genuine UFO capture and subsequently the alien was part of UFO. Dr. Hynek was non-committal but did however sign the report. Also indicated in report that he did not view bodies personally, but viewed photographs and accompanying reports from autopsies.

Other photos dealt with a number of bodies which were vivisectioned in various ways. At one point, a head was removed from body and photographed and autopsy was performed on head. The cranium was opened and brain matter was photographed and evident. Interesting thing about photo was that there was a ridge-bone or dividing partition-type bone running directly through center of skull, from front to back, as though dividing two brains, one from the other. This seemed apparent from the picture. The skin was completely removed from cranial structure and the skull was laid bare as much as possible.

At one point the skull was cut directly in half and photo showed under developed esophagus and nasal cavities. No clear photo of eye orbs as we know them, just photos of complete vivisection of skull itself.

CHAPTER FIFTEEN
FINAL ANALYSIS

This book is called Sensual Alien Encounters for a very specific reason. Based on the evidence it is my belief that a very lobng running breeding program is going on wherein alien beings are cross breeding with mambers of the human race. I make this statement based on the following evidence:

- As observed by Arthur C. Clarke, Any sufficiently advanced technology is indistinguishable from magic.
- Magic is usally associated with the Gods.
- As far back as ancient Sumeria, there are tales of interactions between alien being and humans.
- The ancient Greeks and Romans talk of the "Gods" coming dowen and impregnating human females.

- Many ancient familues in Greece and Roman talk of being dscended form the Gods.
- Most of the ancient Royal Families that ruled much of the planet's surface talk of being descernded from Gods.
- There are numerous contees and abductees who speak of being impregnated by alien visitors.
- In the case of Alexander the Great who spoke ofbeing descnded form the Gods, Ufos helped him in at least two of his greatst battles.
- Numerous individiuals report being molested and or raped by aliens during abductions.
- There are reports of aliens taking semen and ova fro human captives.
- There are many stories, called urban myths of missing persons who disappeared shortly after a UFO contact.
- Animal and human mutilations are much more widespread than we have been led to believe.

Against alien technology the average human is helpless. IN many abductee cases when the aliens have been asked what right they have to kidnap us, they have reporsended, we have the right. If, as stated by Zacharia Sitchin, the aliens created the human race, they may be simly taking samples and making modifications to the human rce to fit some program is research that they have underway.

The final truth will come to light when our government quites classifying everything that happens in the name of National Security and starts telling us the truth. Then we will find out if we are an independent life form or property of some alien zoo keepers.

INDEX

A

Abraham's wife, Sarah, 115
Abzu. *See* House of Far Waters
Achaemenid Empire, 84
Achaemenid Persians, 79
Adapa, 63
Akkadian, 31
Akkadian Empire, 52, 67, 68, 70, 73, 76, 77
Alexander III. *See* Alexander the Great
Alexander the Great, 79, 82, 83, 85, 212
alien abduction, 16
Allagash Abductions, 136
Anânêl, 36
Anchor Bible Dictionary, 11
Angel of Death, 4
Annunaki, 60, 63
Anshar, 33, 60
Anu, 32, 33, 41, 60, 63
Anunnaki, 31, 32, 33, 40
Apostles' Creed, 117
Arâkîba, 35
Araqiel, 36
Archangel Michael, 14
Aristotle, 83
Armaros, 36
Armârôs, 35
Arnold, Kenneth, 17
Asâêl, 35
Assyria, 50, 68, 76, 77
Assyrian, 31, 32, 33
Azazel, 36

B

Babylonia, 54, 68, 75, 76, 77, 78
Babylonian, 31, 32, 33
Baraqel, 36
Barâqîjâl, 35
Batârêl, 35
Beloit College, 142
Berossus, 62
Bezaliel, 36
Bicho Sugador, 182
Bicho Voador, 182
Black Knight, 34
Black, Colonel Robert, 190
Black, Jeremy, 32
Book of Daniel, 34
Book of Enoch, 34, 35, 38
Book of Raziel, 36, 37
Book of Revelation, 14
Books of Enoch, 34
Boston, 34
British UFO Research Association, 103, 104
Brown-Driver-Briggs Lexicon, 10
BUFORA, 103, 104, 106, 119, 126, 149, 154, 157, 160

C

Canaan, 9
Cargo Cults, 12
cattle mutilations, 167, 171, 172, 176, 178
Cavan, Ireland, 169
Chaldea, 48
Chazaqiel, 36
Chupacabra, 170, 171
Clark's Third Law, 112
Clarke, Adam, 10
Close Encounters of the Fifth Kind, 90
Close Encounters of the First Kind, 89
Close Encounters of the Fourth Kind, 89
Close Encounters of the Second Kind, 89
Close Encounters of the Third Kind, 89

Coxon, P. W., 11
Cro-Magnon Man, 23, 26
Cyclops skeletons, 143

D

Dânêl, 35
Darius III, 84
Darwin's Theory, 28
Dead Sea Scrolls, 15
Deluge, 9
deMenocal, Peter B., 70
Demerest, Janet, 160
demons, 14, 16
Diadochi, 85
Dictionary of Deities and Demons in the Bible, 11
Dilmun, 51, 63
DNX Corp, 174
Drake, W. Raymond, 85

E

Ea, 63
Egypt, 69, 75, 78, 79, 80, 83, 146
El Paso, 11
English, Bill, 185
Enki, 41, 63
Enlil, 33, 41
Enoch, 34, 35, 36, 37, 38, 39, 40
Epic of Creation, 33
Epic of Gilgamesh, 33
Eridu, 33, 52, 60, 63
Eurystheus, 91
Ezekiel, 10, 87
Êzêqêêl, 35

F

fallen angels, 12, 13, 15, 16, 17, 35, 36, 40
Fallen Ones, 43
Fort Aztalan, 145

G

Gadreel, 36, 37
Genesis, 9, 11, 38, 42, 58, 59, 110, 143
Girdlestone, Robert Baker, 10
Green, Anthony, 32
Grigori, 38, 39, 40
Grudge/Blue Book Report 13, 188, 190, 191
Guildford, Great Britain, 170

H

Hagar, 115
Hairy Dwarfs, 139
Haskell County, Texas, 171
Hendel, Robert, 10
Hess, Richard, 11
heteropaternal superfecundation, 91
Hill, Betty and Barney, 93
Holzer, Hans, 131
Homo Habilis, 21
Homo sapiens, 22, 26, 27, 28
Hopkinsville Goblins, 139, 141
Hudnall, Ken, 11

I

Igigi, 32, 34
India, 76, 81, 82, 84, 85
Indus Valley Civilization, 81
Iphicles, 91

J

Jacobs, David M., 119
Jefferies, Anne, 92
Jesus, 14, 111, 116, 117
Johnson, Ted, 121
Jômjâêl, 36
Jubilees, 36, 37
Judgment Day, 35

K

Ken Hudnall Show, 185, 187
Ki, 33, 60
Kishar, 33, 60
Kokabiel, 37
Kôkabîêl, 35
Kurz, Shane, 130

L

Lahamu, 33
Lahmu, 33
Lake Delavan, Wisconsin, 141
Lake Mills, 145
Leviticus, 168
Library of Ashurbanipal, 63
London Daily Mail, 169
Lord of light, 39
Louette, Sgt. Jonathan P., 176
Lucifer, 12

M

Marduk, 33, 41, 42
Marrs, Jim, 56
Mât Akkadî, 76
McNeil, William H., 20
Meng Zhaoguo, 133, 135
Mercer Dictionary of the Bible, 40
Middle Kingdom, 79
Morgan, Karen, 160, 161
Moses, 111, 112, 114
MUFON, 177
Murphy, Jane, 97, 118
mutilation of cattle, 167, 171

N

Neanderthal Man, 21
Nephilim, 9, 10, 11, 12, 16, 17, 30, 35, 38, 43, 58, 59, 149
Neptune, 40, 59
New Kingdom, 79
New York Times, 142, 144, 148

Nibiru, 40, 42
Nicene Creed, 117
Ninhursag, 41
Noah, 16, 17, 35
Nordics, 152
Numbers, 9

O

Oannes, 13, 30, 62, 63
Old Kingdom, 69, 72, 79
Omega Press, 3

P

P. W. Coxon, 11
Parker, Will, 157
Penemue, 37
Philip II, 83
Planet X. *See* Nibru
Pluto, 59
Princess of Aztalan, 146, 148

Q

Quetzalcoatl, 48

R

RAF Chicksands, 187
Râmêêl, 35
Râmîêl, 35
Red Flag logging camp, 133
Repeller of the Amorites, 73
Revelations, 110
Roslyn Institute, 174

S

Samsâpêêl, 36
Samyaza, 35, 37
Sargon of Akkad, 68, 77
Sariel, 37
Sariêl, 36
Satan, 14, 15, 17

Satarêl, 36
Sêmîazâz, 35
Shamsiel, 37
Sitchin, Zacharia, 12, 31, 40, 62
sleep paralysis, 16
Smithsonian Institution, 144, 147
Stringfield, Leonard H., 176
Sumerian King List, 70
Sumerians, 13

T

Tâmîêl, 35
Tell Brak, 72
Tell Leilan, 70, 72
Texas
    El Paso, 3, 4
The Observer, 174
Tiamat, 34
Tûrêl, 36
Tyre, 86, 87

U

Uanna, 63
Ubaidians, 50

Uranus, 59
Uriel, 35, 36, 37

V

Villas Boas, Antonio, 93

W

Wang. Connie, 4
watchers, 34
White Sands Missile Test Range, 176, 202
Wisconsin Decatur Republican, 147

Y

Yeqon, 37

Z

Zaqîêl, 36
Zohar, 36, 37

www.ingramcontent.com/pod-product-compliance
Lightning Source LLC
Chambersburg PA
CBHW071611080526
44588CB00010B/1094